THE MIGHTY MULE

BROUGHT TO YOU BY

The books created by Equine Heritage Institute are designed to preserve the history and majesty of the horse. Our goal is to find, understand, and pass on the valuable data about equine use and its influence on humanity. The Equine Heritage Institute is a not for profit 503(c) and 100% of all proceeds from the sale of books, services, and products support Equine Heritage Institute's mission.

To make a donation to EHI, please visit www.ehi-donations.com

SPECIAL THANKS TO OUR TEAM

Mary Chris Foxworthy, Research Writer

Mary Chris' grandfather owned one of the last creameries in the United States that still used horse-drawn milk wagons. This sparked her life-long love affair with horses and passion for keeping horse history alive. After graduating from college with a degree in Food Science and Communications, Mary Chris bought her very first horse with her first paycheck. Since then, she has served on the board of various equine associations and held a judge's card in Carriage Driving. She is known for her work in the Gloria Austin Collection, and has published and presented numerous equine educational programs. She has written for several equine publications and won an award from American Horse Publications for one of her articles. Mary Chris is an active exhibitor in Carriage Driving and Dressage. Along with her husband, she enjoys spending time with their horses (two Morgans and a PRE), a bouncing Bearded Collie and two adult children and one grandchild.

Abby David, Graphic Designer

Abby David's family has roots in the Walking Horse tradition and she grew up hearing tales of Ole Tobe and Pete the mule's antics, holiday wagon decorations, and trick riding. In her teens she spent her summers boarding the neighbors horses and playing at barrel racing in the back paddock with Thunder. She landed a job as a Graphic Designer at The Arts Center of Cannon County in 2004 and has worked in the print and digital mass communications industry continuously. Since marrying into a family in the racehorse business, she has enjoyed exploring a whole new world of horses and wearing big fancy hats. She also enjoys dancing in all it's forms and teaches in her local community. Read her family mule stories on pages 115-121, and 124.

Gloria Austin's Collection of Books

www.GloriaAustin.com

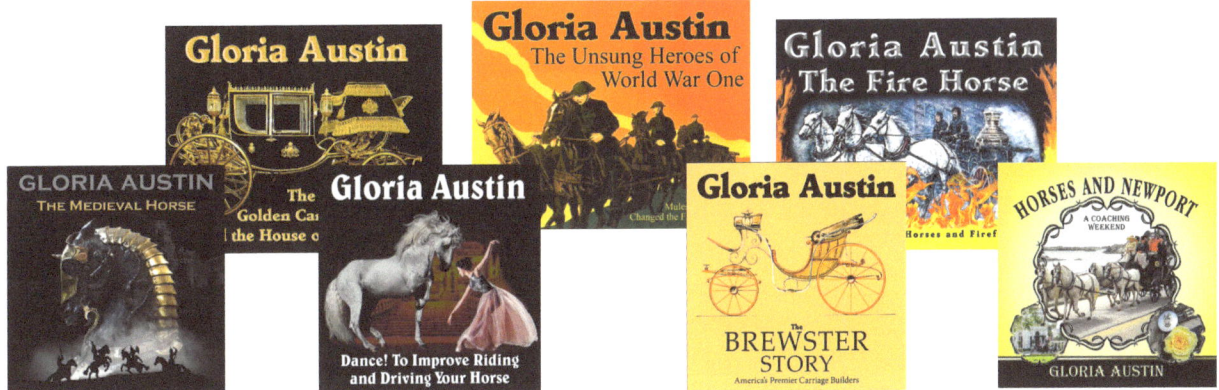

ENJOY OUR OTHER BOOKS

- The Brewster Story
- Carriage Lamps
- Gloria Austin's Carriage Collection
- A Glossary of Harness Parts
- Equine Elegance
- The Fire Horse
- Horse Basics 101
- The Unsung Heros of World War One
- The Horse, History, and Human Culture
- Horse Symbolism
- Horses of the Americas
- A Drive Through Time: Carriages, Horses, and History
- The Medieval Horse
- Speak Your Horse's Language
- Tea: Steeped in Tradition
- Woman and Horses
- The Golden Carriage and the House of Hapsburg
- Horses and Newport
- A Cookbook for Horse Lovers
- Dance! To Improve Riding and Driving
- Westward Ho!

Brought To You By The Equine Heritage Institute

THE MIGHTY MULE
By: Gloria Austin President of Equine Heritage Institute, Inc. (EHI)

First Publish October 15, 2020
Copyright © 2020 by Equine Heritage Institute, Inc.

All rights reserved. No part of this publication may be reproduced, distributed, or transmitted in any form or by any means, including photocopying, recording, or other electronic or mechanical methods, without the prior written permission of the publisher, except in the case of brief quotations embodied in critical reviews, submitted stories in the Mule Stories Chapter, and certain other noncommercial uses permitted by copyright law. For permission requests, write to the publisher, addressed "Attention: Permissions Coordinator," at the address below.

Gloria Austin Carriage Collection, LLC; Equine Heritage Institute, Inc.
3024 Marion County Road Weirsdale, FL 32195 Office: (352) 753-2826 Fax: (352) 753-6186

Ordering Information:
Quantity sales: Special discounts are available on quantity purchases by corporations, associations, and others. For details, contact the publisher at the address above.
Printed in the United States of America First Edition
ISBN: Print, 978-1-951895-09-9, E-book, 978-1-951895-10-5

TABLE OF CONTENTS

Mule Qualities 8
Mule Basics 8
    What is a Mule? 8
    Mule Terminology 12
    "Making "a Mule - The Formula 16
    "Making" a Mule - Meet the Horse 18
    "Making" a Mule - Meet the Donkey 20
    Mule Traits - Characteristics and Conformation 24
    Mule Traits - Differences: Mule vs Horse 26
    Mule Versatility 30
    Mule Tack 36
    Training a Mule 40
Mule History 43
    Mules in Ancient Times 43
    Mules in the Middle Ages and Renaissance 46
    Mules Throughout Europe 51
    Mules in the New World 54
    Mules in America 56
Mules in the Modern Era 75
Mule Stories 85
    Sir Gawain and the Bridleless Mule 85
    Mule Bombs of Valverde 86
    Smokey Joe 88
    Zhang Guolao and His Mule 89
    Duldul 89
    When a horse lover opens her heart to mules 90
    Roy the Big Red Mule 92
    Mule Days 93
    The Great American Horse Race 94
    The Funeral of Alexander the Great 98
    Flying Mules 100
    Honky 101
    The Charge of the Mule Brigade 102
    The Real Civil War Mule Brigades 104
    Bess - The Mine Mule 106
    Francis the Talking Mule 110
    Festus and Ruth 112
    Three Mules 114
    Ole Pete 115
    Puckett General Store 120
    Roanie - Spirit Led 122
    Ole Tobe 124
    Sterlin the Appy Mule 125
    Lightning 126
The Joys of Mule Ownership 127
What is Your Mule Personality 129
My Mule Story 132
Sources 136

The Horse

"We have had 6,000 years of history with the domesticated horse and only 100 years with the automobile."

Gloria Austin

MULE QUALITIES

There are so many ways to describe a mule: loyal, steadfast, strong, reliable, calm, tolerant, intelligent, stubborn, sensible, patient and much more. Some even say that a mule has a sense of humor. What adjective best describes the mule? By the time you are finished reading this book we hope you will come to know, love and respect "The *Mighty* Mule".

MULE BASICS - What Is A Mule?

Horses and donkeys are different species, with different numbers of chromosomes. However, they have all evolved from the same family called equidae. These species all belong to a sub-family of animals called equus. The mule is a cross between a donkey stallion (called a jack) and a horse mare. Hinnies are just the opposite - a stallion horse crossed to a donkey mare (called a jennet). A mule or hinny may be a male or a female. Sometimes males are called Johns and females are called Mollies. Mules and hinnies have 63 chromosomes, a mixture of the horse's 64 and the donkey's 62. The different structure and number usually prevents the chromosomes from pairing up properly and creating successful embryos, rendering most mules infertile. A very few (about 1 in 1 million) mares have had foals. No male has ever sired a foal.

Mules come in every size and shape imaginable; miniature to mammoth. The offspring of a donkey/horse cross can vary from very large draft mules over 17 hands high to the tiniest of mules under 36 inches The rarer hinnies are often said to be more horselike than the mule, but more often it is impossible to tell them apart. Hinnies may

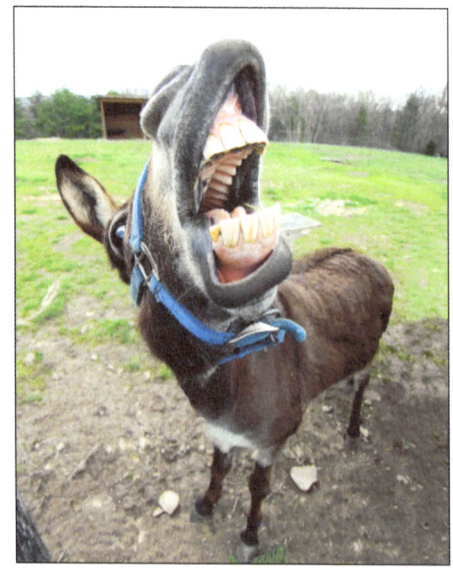

If you want to know what part of you needs more work, ask a mule and he will show you.

tend to be slightly smaller, simply because of the fact that most donkeys are smaller than horses. The build of the mule is a combination of both parents. Mule's ears are usually somewhat smaller than a donkey's, longer but the same shape as the horse parents. The head, hip and legs usually take after the donkey. Mules' hooves are less likely to split or crack and can withstand mountainous trails and rocky farm soil. The eyes are more almond-shaped than the horse; inherited from the D-shaped eye socket of the donkey. Male mules may have more prominent brow ridges like those of most donkey jacks. The neck is straight and has little arch, even in mules from Arab mares. The overall body shape will be dependent on the conformation of both parents. Due to hybrid vigor, the mule has the possibility of growing taller than either parent. The skin of a mule is less sensitive than that of a horses and more resistant to sun and rain. This makes mules a dependable option for owners who work outside in harsh weather and strong sunlight. The mule will have "combination hair", usually a thin forelock, coarse mane hair and a tail more like the horse parent. Mules usually have brown or tan-colored points. Mules can be any of the colors that either horses or donkeys come in, along with some unique variations of their own. The only colors mules do not come in is true horse pinto; due to the genetic factoring of these colors, there are some mules who are close to, but not quite, tobiano patterned and none recorded in overo. Mules from Appaloosa mares often have extremely loud patterns, with spots enlarging or "skewing" in variants of the horse Appaloosa. Mules try their best to imitate the donkey's bray, but most have a unique sound that is a combination of a horse and a donkey. Mules require less food and have more stamina than horses of the same weight and height, making them resilient working animals in some of the harshest environments.

A Leopard Appaloosa Mule

Draft Mules

Although the average lifespan for mules is between 35 and 40 years, some mules have been known to live until 50, especially if well looked after. *(cited from: http://www.lovelongears.com/about_mules.html and https://spana.org/blog/what-is-a-mule-13-things-you-didnt-know/)*

Worldwide there are approximately:
- 55 million horses
- 44 million donkeys
- 13 million mules and hinnies

That means there are 57 million equine with long ears!

More than 90% of those long ears are working animals in developing regions of the world

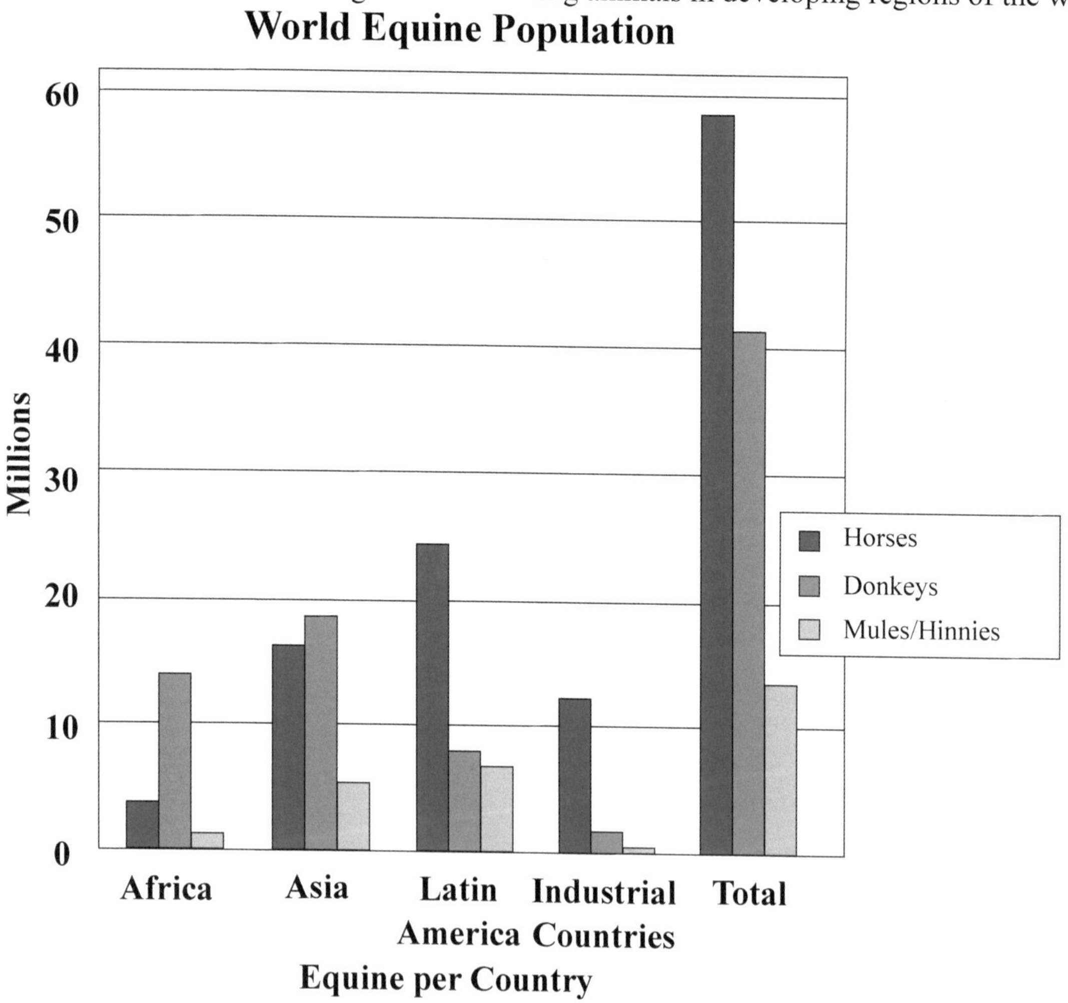

World Equine Population

(cited from: Amy K. McLean, NC State University Equine Extension/ Animal Science Raleigh, NC)

Mules and donkeys are often used as beasts of burden - even living burdens! Mule and donkey nannies are often used when grazing animals are moved from high pastures down to the plains. Newborn lambs are unable to make the journey on their own so they ride in pouches on a specially made saddle. At rest stops, lambs are returned to their mothers for a meal and some nuzzling.

Mule Terminology

American Mammoth Jackstock: a breed of North American donkey, descended from large donkeys imported to the United States from about 1785. George Washington, with Henry Clay and others, bred for an ass that could be used to produce strong work mules. Washington was offering his jacks for stud service by 1788.

Ass: The correct term for the animal commonly know as the donkey, burro or jackstock. The term comes from the original Latin term, Asinus. The scientific term for these animals is equus asinus. The term fell into disrepute through confusion with the indelicate term "arse" meaning the human backside. The difference between asses and horses is a species difference; different species but closely related and able to interbreed to a degree.

Bell tails: When the Army used mules in service. A green mule had its tail shaved. By the time the mule was broke to pack, a 'bell' was trimmed in the tail. Once broke to drive, a second bell was added below the first. Broke to ride, a third tassel was trimmed below the second. Thus, a three-bell mule was a well-schooled animal. One might say a "3-bell mule" is a mule with a PhD.

Burro: a word taken directly from Spain. It means the common, everyday working donkey found in Spain and Mexico. It came into usage in the Western United States. As a general rule, the term burro is heard west of the Mississippi and the term donkey, east of the Mississippi.

Coletta: a chair, litter, or other contrivance fitted to the back or pack saddle of a mule for carrying travelers in mountainous districts or for the transportation of the sick and wounded of an army

Cotton mule: a smaller, lighter type of mule (larger than a mining mule, smaller than a sugar mule) often used for plowing light soil - a now obsolete term as, these days, most people refer to their mule's type according to the mother's breed (i.e. a Thoroughbred mule)

Donkey markings

Donkey: taken from England, the derivation is uncertain, but most authorities think that the name comes from dun (the usual color) and the suffix "ky," meaning small; thus "a little dun animal"

Draft mule: a mule out of a draft horse mare - This term was part of the old categories of mules (cotton mules, sugar mules, etc.) but remains in use today.

Hinny: the hybrid offspring of a donkey mother and a horse father – the opposite way round to a mule

Horse Mule: the proper term for the male mule

Jack: intact male donkey, thus the often used term jackass

Jack Stock: the term for plural of the American Mammoth Jack and Jennet. These animals are properly termed asses and not donkeys, and never called burros. They are one of the largest of the types of the ass species.

Draft Mules

Jenney: female donkey; the correct term for the female of the species. The more commonly used term is jenny, which is considered correct in non-technical use.

John: a male mule, also sometimes referred to as a horse mule

Mare Mule: term for a female mule

Markings: In addition to The Cross, many donkeys have dark markings on the ears, as "garters" around the legs, or as "zippers" down the inside forelegs. Small black spots on the sides of the throat, called collar buttons, may also be seen, as well as dark line (ventral stripe) down the belly. When registering donkeys, white points are so universally normal that only the absence of them is to be noted. It is normal for a donkey to have short, fine, light colored hair on the muzzle, ringing the eyes, on the belly and inside the legs. A donkey that does not have these points is seen as unusual but is not uncommon. The donkey usually passes the light points on to the mule, although they may appear brown or tan instead of off-white or pale gray like in the donkey. Many mules will have crosses and leg stripes as well. The crosses of mules usually differ from those on donkeys, with the shoulder stripe being very wide, or faded, as in shadow.

Miniature Mule: bred from various types of miniature donkeys and horses

Molly: a female mule, also sometimes referred to as a mare mule

Mule: hybrid of jack and a horse mare

Mule bars: bars of a saddle that have been specifically designed to accommodate the straight back of a mule. A mule is also part donkey and the donkey's bone structure is fundamentally different than a horse's. The mule gets his bone structure, or skeletal structure, from the donkey so a horse saddle will not fit a mule.

Mule sense: Common sense!

Muleskinner: a muleteer or mule-driver. Mule skinners (or mule drivers) and their complements, the bullwhackers (freighters with oxen), flourished from the 1850s through the 1870s, when millions of tons of freight were being pulled by mules and oxen across the Great Plains. In the early 1860s the great firm of Russell, Majors and Waddell operated 6,250 wagons and 75,000 oxen pulling freight west of the Missouri River. Mules and mule skinners were probably as numerous as oxen and bullwhackers at that time.

Muleteer: a professional mule handler. This term derives from the Middle French word for mule driver and is widely used in Europe.

Mule train: a long line of mules, either pulling a load or carrying pack

Pack Mule: bred from mares with some draft blood or of heavy work types rather than for saddle type.

Pit mule: mules that are generally pony-sized and used for working underground, although the name was also sometimes applied to the larger mules who worked on the surface. They are the smallest of the old categories of mules, the next size up being the cotton mule.

Pack Mule: The animals used 100 years ago to build Southern California Edison's hydroelectric system still are needed for some power projects in the wilderness.

Pit Mule

Saddle mule: a mule suitable for riding

String: a collective term for the mules in a pack team

Sugar Mule: larger than a cotton mule and smaller than a draft mule. These animals were solidly built and got their names due to being suitable for working on the sugar plantations.

The Cross: refers to a line of darker hair starting at the tip of the head and running to the end of the tail on a donkey. This is crossed at the withers with another darker line of hair (the shoulder stripe) forming a cross. The shoulder stripe may be long, very short, thin, wide, fading or dashed, but nearly all donkeys have some form of this marking. The exceptions are the Mammoth donkeys, which have been bred away from this marking, and true black animals where the cross is not visible. Even spotted animals or white-appearing donkeys may have partial or faint crosses. This trait is very dominant. (cited from: http://mulography.co.uk/a-glossary-of-mule-terminology/ and http://www.cvm.missouri.edu/org/muleclub/mule.html and http://imh.org/exhibits/online/breeds-of-the-world/europe/mule/)

Sugar Mule: "Restless" making his rounds pulling the sweep to grind sugar cane in Tallahassee, FL - 1962

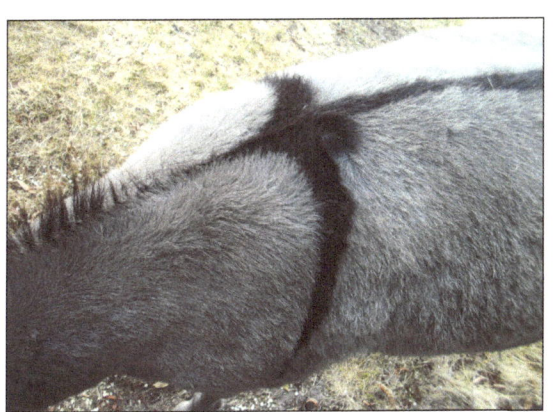

A mule-powered cane mill producing syrup from sugarcane at the second annual Texas Folklife Festival - 1973
[Mule-Powered Cane Mill], photograph, [1973-09-07..1973-09-09]; (https://texashistory.unt.edu/ark:/67531/metapth227370/m1/1/: accessed June 11, 2020), University of North Texas Libraries, The Portal to Texas History, https://texashistory.unt.edu; crediting UT San Antonio Libraries Special Collections.

"Making" A Mule - The Formula

Under conditions of domestication it is possible to obtain hybrids between equid species. There are records of onager/horse and zebra/horse crosses but the cross that has been most significant in human history is one between donkeys and horses. This cross produces the Mule.

Onagers are a species of Asian wild ass that ranges from northwest Iran to Turkmenistan. They are part of the horse family along with donkeys and zebras. Unlike their cousins, though, onagers have never been domesticated because they are notoriously hard to tame. They are some of the world's fastest mammals, able to run 40 - 70 mph, which is pretty impressive! The ancient Roman Legions are thought to have used these animals to pull their war machines. Onagers were previously considered a species, Equus onager, but have since been included as a subspecies of kulans, Equus hemionus.

Onager

Relatively few hinnies (stallion horse and donkey jenny) are bred. The reason for this is not because hinnies are inherently less useful, but because they are harder to create. Fertility rates from stallion / jenny matings are lower because it is harder to breed a hybrid if the chromosome numbers are lower in the female (horses have 64 chromosomes while donkeys have 62).

There is some thought that the animals pulling the Sumerian chariots in the Standard of Ur are onagers or a mule from a horse/onager cross

Zebra

Zebra horse cross

Donkey

Mule: Donkey (Jack) stallion + horse mare

Horse Stallion

Hinny: Donkey (Jennet) mare + horse stallion

"Making" A Mule - Meet The Horse

The mother of a mule - the horse mare - can be any breed and size of horse. The resulting mule can be a Quarter Horse mule, a Belgian mule, an Appaloosa mule, a Tennessee Walker mule, a Miniature mule… the list goes on. Whatever breed you particularly like can be used to raise that "type" of mule; they can originate from any horse breed. You can create the mule you want in one generation!

The bad reputation that still precedes mules in many areas of North America does not come from the donkey. On the contrary, it is a carry-over from when horse mares that were not desirable as horse breeding stock were bred to a jack to produce something of value. The result was often an animal that could work but carried the same undesirable disposition as its mother, and was generally difficult to handle. Good mares were not bred to good jacks, thus the mules that were raised for a time in the development of the west were often cantankerous and unpredictable. Thankfully, those days have passed and now it is becoming more predominant to raise mules out of only good, proven mares. The result is mules that excel in beauty and disposition. *(cited from: https://thefarmatwalnutcreek.com/horses-draft-mule.html)*

The Missouri Mule is the state animal of Missouri. It is a cross between a mare of a draft breed and a Mammoth Jack.

Appaloosa Mule: dam = Appaloosa Horse

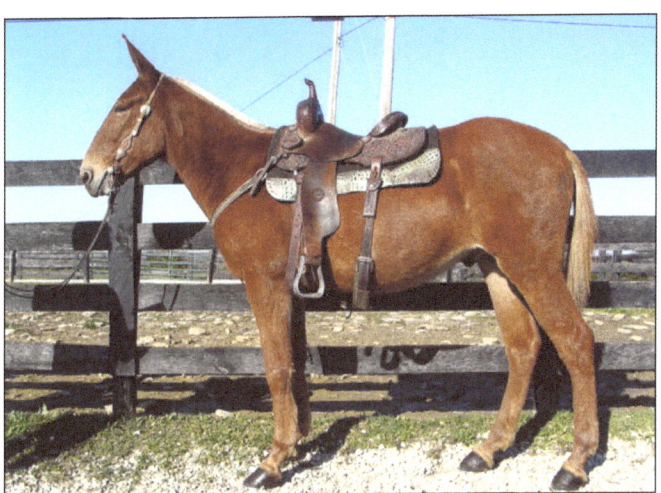

Quarter Mule: dam = Quarter Horse

Arabian Mule: dam = Arabian Horse

Gaited Mule: dam usually a Missouri Foxtrotter, Tennessee Walker, Saddlebred, Paso Fino or other gaited horse. The result of these breedings will produce a mule that will do a flat walk, running walk, rack or other gaits.

Draft Mule: dam = Belgian Horse

"Making" A Mule - Meet The Donkey

The father of a mule - the donkey jack - can be any size or breed of donkey.

The Mammoth donkey, the largest, is in demand for saddle and draft mule production. This breed is the largest donkey in the world. Jacks must stand 56" or more, and jennets must be 54" and up. The correct name for this breed is American Standard, but the common name is Mammoth, which helps avoid confusion with standard donkeys.

Standard donkeys can also be used in saddle mule production. Most donkeys in the world are in this size range. Often called burros, they stand between 36.01" and 48" at the withers and are further divided into:
Small Standard—36.01" to 40"
Standard—40.01" to 48"
Large Standard—48.01" to 54" (jennets) and 48.01" to 56" (jacks).

Donkeys that originally imported from Sicily and Sardinia and are colloquially referred to as Sicilian donkeys and are more commonly known as miniature donkeys. Sicilian donkeys actually arrived in Sicily via their native North Africa. A miniature donkey can be crossed with a miniature horse to produce a miniature mule. A miniature donkey must be less than 36" at the withers to be registered as miniature by the American Donkey and Mule Society. *(cited from: https://www.ruralheritage.com/mule_paddock/donkeys.htm)*

Somaliens (Africa)

Hemione Onager (Asia)

Pega (Brazil)

Criollo (Colombia)

Poitou (France)

Amiata (Italy)

Asinara (Italy)

Martina Franca (Italy)

Ragusano (Italy)

Romagnolo (Italy)

Andaluz (Spain)

Catalán (Spain)

Zamorano (Spain)

Mammoth (USA)

Pinto Americano (USA)

The most probable ancestor of the domestic donkey (Equus asinus) is the Nubian subspecies of African wild ass; however, the history of its domestication is poorly known. The earliest known remains of the domestic donkey date to the fourth millennium BC from a site at Ma'adi, Lower Egypt. It is probable that peoples in Nubia first developed the domestic donkey as a beast of burden. The tame donkey was easily led by any type of halter available and could be trained to follow a route on its own. Donkey domestication resulted in increased mobility of pastoral peoples and perhaps contributed to a true nomadic lifestyle in which whole families, rather than just the men, could follow their flocks from pasture to pasture. Donkeys were kept in great herds in ancient Egypt. In the tombs of the Dynasty IV (ca. 2675-2565 BC) there are indications that wealthy and powerful people possessed droves of over a thousand donkeys. In addition to their use as a pack animal, donkeys were employed to tread seeds into the fertile Nile floodplain and to thresh the harvest. Elsewhere, mares were kept as dairy animals. Donkey's milk, higher both in sugar and protein content than cow's milk, was used as food, as medicine and as a cosmetic to promote a white skin. The donkey was dispersed out of the Nile Valley and eventually reached all habitable continents. *(cited from: http://imh.org/exhibits/online/breeds-of-the-world/africa/donkey/)*

There are some people that think making a super mule by using an onager would be amazing - but trying to catch and breed an onager might be even more amazing!

The Poitou donkey *(left)* is used for breeding huge draft mules called Mule Poitevine or Poitou Mule *(right)* from a breed of draft horse called the Poitevin mulassier *(center)*.

Poitou Donkey   **Poitevin Mulassier**   **Mule Poitevine or Poitou Mule**

Miniature donkey *(left)* bred with miniature horse *(center)* to produce miniature mule *(right)*.

Miniature Donkey

Miniature Horse

Miniature Mule

Mammoth Jackstock *(left)* bred with Percheron draft horse *(center)* to produce draft mule *(right -This is the famous John Henry - "one cool mule")*

Mammoth Jackstock

Percheron Draft Horse

Produce Draft Mule

Mule Traits
CHARACTERISTICS AND CONFORMATION

Horse + Donkey = Mule

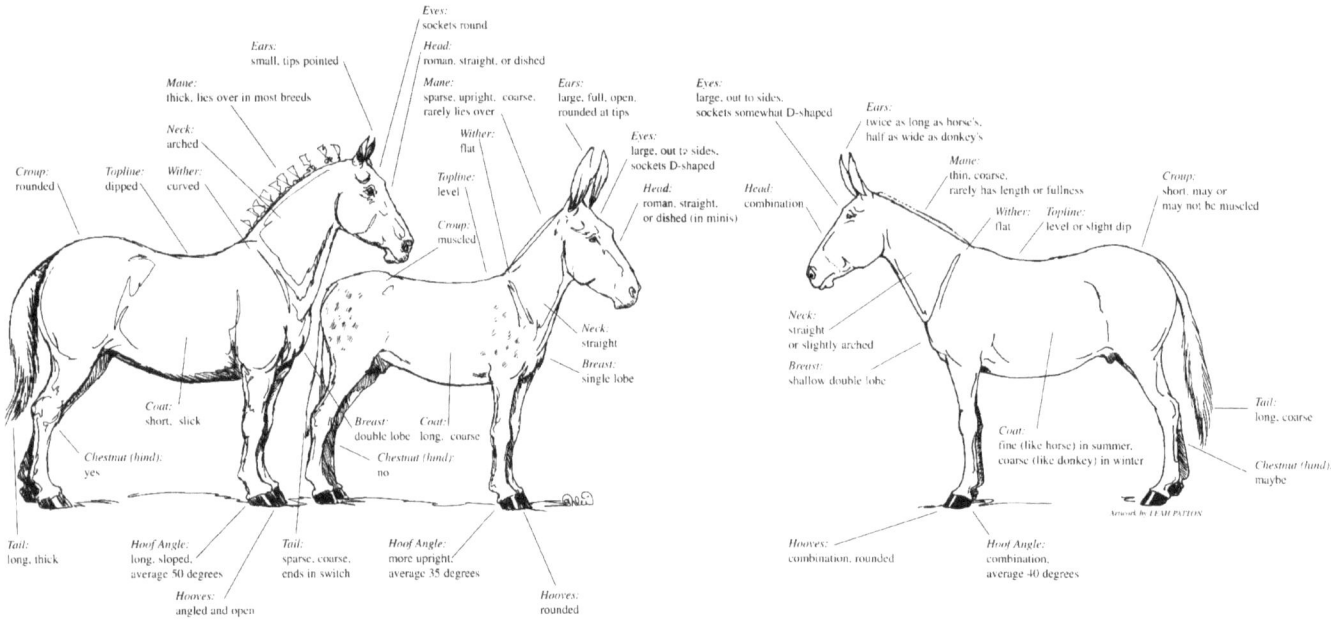

- The mule is similar to both donkey and horse, not only in terms of appearance, but also in nature and behavior.
- It has a short thick head, short mane, thin limbs and small hooves, like that of a donkey.
- The head, hip and legs usually take after the jack.
- Mules do not have pronounced arches to the neck, even from breeds such as Arabians or Warmbloods.
- Mules resembles horses in terms of height, neck, croup, teeth and body shape.
- Mules are highly patient, sober and tolerant like a donkey.
- A mule is courageous, vigorous and strong like a horse.
- The mule comes in a variety of colors, like black, grey, sorrel and bay. The less common colors are white, palomino, buckskin, roans and dun.
- The mule does not sound like either of its parents. Its cry is mixture of a horse's and donkey's sound; the sound is similar to that of a donkey with the whining characteristics of those of a horse.

- The mule's size and its capacity to do work depend on its breeding. It can be light, medium or heavy weight, depending on the mare used for breeding.
- All mules and most of the hinnies are infertile in nature. However, several hinnies have been able to reproduce offspring, when mated with a purebred horse or donkey.
- A mule has hard skin, which is not sensitive to sun and rain.
- Mules have hard hooves.
- The mule can carry large weights on its back. Generally, a mule can carry "dead weight" up to 20% of its body weight which consist of non-living things. When it comes to live weight, like a rider, it can carry up to 30% of its body weight.
- Mules are naturally resistant to diseases and insects.
- Mules can strike with any of its hooves in any direction, including sideways.
- A mule is more intelligent in comparison to its parents.
- A mule is highly curious in nature and generally does not allow the rider to lead it into any dangerous path.
- Mules tend to eat less than a horse of the same size.

(cited from: https://paintedqhfarm.weebly.com/mule-facts.html)

Mule Traits
DIFFERENCES: MULE VS. HORSE

Mules endure heat better than horses do.
It has been scientifically proven that the donkey is similar to the camel in its ability, when water starved, to drink only enough water to replace lost body fluids. Most mules inherit this ability.

Mules have fewer feeding problems than horses do.
Many farmers keep their draft and work mules together in pens with feed available at all times, yet the mules rarely overeat to the point of colic or founder. Mules from pony mares, however, may grass or grain or road founder, so the idea that a mule never founders is not true. Mules require no fancy hay-just plain, clean, fresh hay suitable for equines. People who buy cheaper weedy hay find that their mules clean out the weeds first.

Mules eat less than horses do.
Mules that are not working usually don't need grain at all. Good pasture or clean hay is the usual maintenance ration. When mules are working, their grain ration is usually about 1/3 less than that of a horse of the same size. Of course, a mule must be fed enough for its size, its metabolism and the work it is doing. Research has shown that donkeys have a slower gastrointestinal tract time, meaning what they eat stays in their digestive track longer compared to a horse, therefore they can maximize digestion and possibly nutrient absorption.

Sure-footed Smokey Joe (meet him later in this book)

Mules rarely have hoof problems.
Mules naturally have small, upright, boxy feet which is part of the secret of their surefootedness. Mules that work on pavement or stony ground are often shod, but most pleasure animals, or mules that work on softer ground, never see a shoe. Regular hoof trimming keeps them just fine. Their feet are strong, tough, flexible, and usually not as brittle and shelly as those of a horse. They have less of a problem with splitting, chipping, and contracted heels.

Mules are surefooted and careful.
Their surefootedness is partly physical and partly psychological. On the physical side, the mule has a narrower body than a horse of the same height and weight. He gets this from the ass side of the family. His legs are strong and his feet are small and neat. This narrow structure and small hoof configuration enable him to place his feet carefully and neatly. On the psychological side, mules have a tendency to assess situations and act according to their views (most of which have to do with self preservation). A mule will trust its own judgment before it trusts yours.

Mules live longer productive lives than horses do.
Farm mules average 18 years to a horse's 15 years. When the mule is a companion animal doing lighter work and getting better medical care, better feed and good management, the mule can give its owner good riding at age 30; 40-year-old retirees are not at all uncommon.

Mules can be handled in large groups more easily than horses.
Mules can be kept on farms, 30 or 40 to a group, or up to 500 in a feeding pen, without the injuries or other consequences commonly seen with horses.

Mules have a strong sense of self preservation.
This is one good reason why mules physically last longer than horses do. If they are overheated, overworked or overused for any reason, mules will either slow down to a safe pace or stop completely. Mules are not stubborn. Neither are donkeys; they are just more sensible than people sometimes. The facts that mules are inclined not to panic, that they think about what is happening to them, and they take care of their own physical well being prevents many accidents that might happen if they were horses.

Mules incur fewer veterinary expenses.
It seems odd and unprovable, but to the confirmed mule owner, a horse seems to be a vet bill waiting for a place to happen. Hybrid vigor accounts for a good deal of the mule's sturdy health. The toughness of the ass accounts for the other aspects. Perhaps the instinct of self preservation that shows up in such diverse ways as not drinking or eating too much when hot or not panicking when caught in barbed wire, accounts for the rest. This is not to say that mules never get sick, injured or otherwise "damaged." It is just that they are tougher than horses and they take care of themselves better.

Mules excel in physical soundness.
Mules last longer, are more maintenance free and are less expensive at the vet's office than horses are. Leg problems are far less likely in a mule than in a horse and when leg problems do occur, they are far less severe. "Why do they stay sound?" wonders Robert Miller, DVM. "Seeking answers... equine practitioners exposed daily to the tragedy of lameness in beautiful horses, look at the mules, run their hands down the tough little legs, and wonder." Not only legs, but wind, "innards," and all other parts of the mule including his hide are tougher and more durable than comparable parts of the horse. Hybrid vigor explains a lot of this; the tough physical and mental qualities of the donkey explain the rest.

Mules move differently than horses.
While you might not be able to see the difference between a mule or horse when they are standing still, as soon as they start moving, you can see that they are not the same. Let's first look at shoulder movement. The mule's shoulder moves up and down. When you watch a mule walk, you can actually see the shoulder moving up and down – why? Because they get their bone structure from a donkey and when the donkey walks, his shoulders go up and down. When you watch a horse walk, you'll see that they don't move up and down. The horse shoulders actually move backward and forward. Not only does the mule shoulder move differently than a horse's shoulder, the shape of the shoulder is fundamentally different. When we look at a mule we see that they are V-shaped in the shoulders, they have an hourglass belly and they carry the bulk of their weight down low. Horses, on the other hand, are A-shaped in their shoulders and they carry their weight up high. (*cited from: https://www.muleranch.com/mule-saddle-everything-you-need-to-know/*)

Mules don't look like horses.
This is the thing about a mule that is most obvious to the casual observer - they look different! Well, you see, mule lovers like the look of a mule. They love those magnificent big ears. They love to watch those ears flop in a relaxing rhythm on a placid drive or prick rigidly forward when the mule spots something interesting. Mule owners like the mule's look of strength without bulk. Mule owners know that a mule will draw attention where only the most outstanding and expensive horse will stand out from the crowd.

Mules are loaded with personality.
This is the most difficult thing to define. Yes, mules are intelligent. They can be very decided about how they want to do things. To own one is to love one! (*cited from: https://paintedqhfarm.weebly.com/mule-facts.html*)

The mule bone structure is different from the horse bone structure.
Yes, a mule is part horse. Yes, they look similar. But a mule is also part donkey and the donkey's bone structure is fundamentally different than a horse's. The mule gets his bone structure, or skeletal structure, from the donkey. While what you and I see on the outside may look like the same shape and sizing as a horse, underneath the skin, everything is different.

Morphological Parameters of Mules and Hinnies: Comparing and Contrasting Conformation

Horse: Neck = Middle = Hip, 2:1 ratio

Donkey: Middle > Neck > Hip, 1:1 ratio

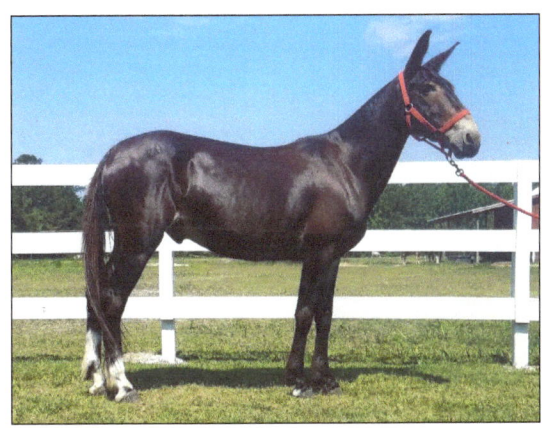

Mule: Middle = Neck > Hip, 2:0,85, p=0.03 ratio

Hinny: Middle = Neck > Hip, 1:1 ratio

(cited from: https://americanmuleassociation.org/differences-with-horses-and-donkeys)

Mule Versatility

Mules can be used in exactly the same sports as horses - under saddle, in harness, for cutting, roping or dressage. In actuality, they have more stamina and can carry more weight than a horse of equal size. This is due to the hybrid vigor

Endurance

Pack Train

Packing

Hunting

Jumping

Dressage

Roping

Reining

Mounted Shooting

Carriage Driving

Farming

Hitch Team

Trail

Pulling

Racing

Barrel Racing

There is one particular aspect where the mule actually outshines the horse and that is high-jumping. Mules have a particular sport all their own called the Coon Hunter's Jump. It stems from the raccoon hunter moving his saddle and pack mules through the woods. Wooden or stone fences could be taken down but wire ones could not. The hunter would flag the fence with his coat or a blanket and jump his string of pack mules over one by one. In the show ring, mules jump a single rail standard to increasing heights. The last clean jump is the winner. Mules only 50 inches tall at the withers have been known to clear jumps of up to 72 inches. These jumps are not from a galloping approach, like Puissance, but from a standing start inside a marked area. Truly a remarkable feat!

Charged with delivering supplies to remote locations where fire crews are working, California mules have been employed during fire season for more than 70 years. The United States Forest Service explained that the "old school technology" that comes from a pack string of mules provides "important support" in fire suppression. A "pack string" refers to a group of mules tied together as a group.

The Forest Service acknowledges that using the mules is becoming a "vanishing skill," but when smoke from a fire limits aircraft support, strings of mules "ensure that we can keep the spike camps supplied." Mules can travel up to 16 miles with 150 pounds of gear or more. Among the supplies they are responsible for bringing are tools, clothing, medical supplies and food.

A diet of weed-free hay, grains and alfalfa cubes gives the mules the stamina they need to complete the arduous work their missions require. Each string of mules includes a pack of 5 to 10 mules. In a single trip, a string of mules can carry an amount of supplies that would require 10 to 12 helicopter flights.

At times, using mule packs is the only choice since there are environmental regulations in certain areas making mules the only resource available. During a 2016 wildfire in the Sespe Wilderness of Los Padres National Forest, wilderness designations that protected special areas of the forest prevented motorized or mechanical transportation from entering the area. Each morning, the pack strings of mules headed out to deliver supplies to firefighters set up in remote areas of the forest where motorized vehicles couldn't deliver supplies.

More than 1,000 mules were used by the United States Forest Service in the 1930s. The force is down to only about 120 mules as of 2018. *(cited from: https://www.newsweek.com/fight-california-wildfires-mules-modern-technology-firefighters-1068010)*

Mule Tack

Mules are built differently than horses due to the influence of the donkey. The donkey gives the mule a broader forehead, larger eyes and a wider base at the ears. The average sized horse brow band is typically too short at the base of the ears for the mule, often resulting in pinching. A brow band that isn't long enough can rub or cut the back of the crown (behind the ears), causing soreness and discomfort for the mule. Often, the throat latch also needs to be a bit longer too. The average mule will take a 19" to 20" brow band. Brow bands are measured at the longest point. Some large mules will take a 22". It is better to have a bigger brow band than too small. *(cited from: https://buckarooleather.com/blogs/buckaroo-johns-blog/learning-how-to-properly-fit-large-horse-mule-tack)*

Mules have a narrow chest and need a type of breast collar that fits up above their shoulders and they usually need an over the neck strap to hold the breast collar up in the best pulling position.

The breast collar is very important. The breast collar and the breeching, together, help keep the saddle in place. The proper breast collar is designed to be V-shape that follows the slope of the mule and donkey shoulder. The breast collar should not be real wide as that would inhibit the shoulder.

Breeching is necessary to support trail work in mountainous conditions. Since mules have a flat back both breeching and breast collars are recommended equipment for all mules ridden on trails.

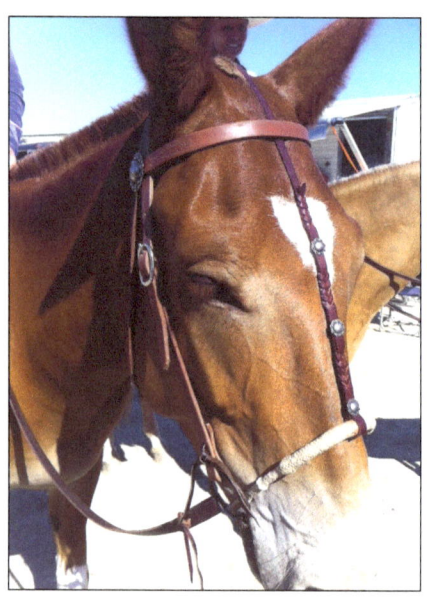

Properly Fitted Headstall

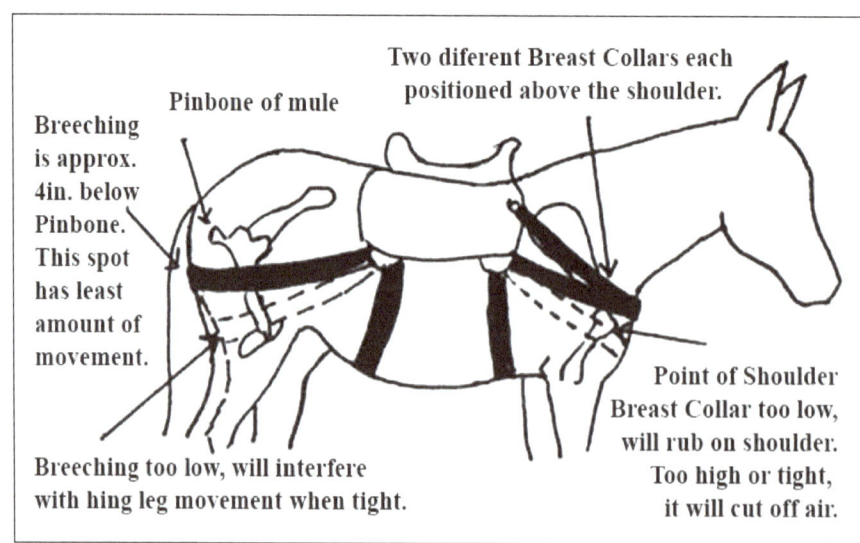

Donkeys and mules are used to carry cargo in many parts of the world and heavy loads are often placed directly on their backs or on ill-fitting pack saddles that often rub against their skin, causing nasty and sometimes life-threatening wounds. However, there is equipment available to prevent this.

There are two types of pack saddles. The sawbuck, also called the crossbuck, sports two Xs made of wood, protruding up from the saddle. The sawbuck requires two cinches to keep it securely attached on the mule. While the Decker saddle, used by the US Forest Service, also contains two wood bars; these bars are not connected by wooden Xs but by D rings. Deckers are generally single-rigged, using just one cinch. The Decker is covered by a padded fabric known as a "half-breed." It contains two boards that lie horizontally along each side of the mule's rib cage. Because of these features, the Decker affords the mule superior back protection. *(cited from: https://animals.mom.me/pack-mule-9165.html)*

Decker Pack Saddle

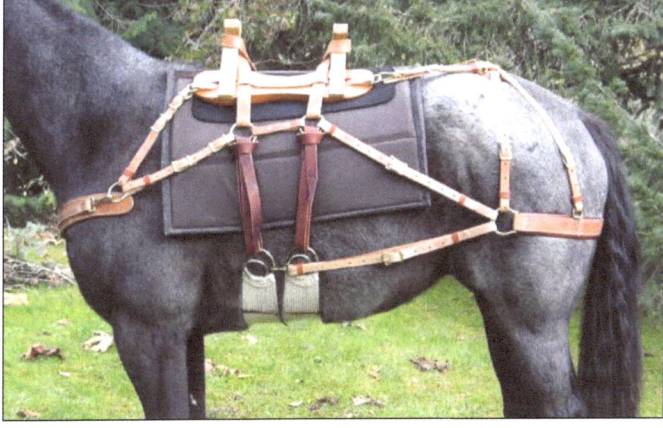
Sawbuck Pack Saddle

The "pannier" refers to any bags or boxes used to cart supplies or equipment. Fabric panniers are easier on the mule, while those made of metal or plastic are better for protecting your belongings. Panniers sport loops which you can place on the crossbucks saddle or hook or thread through D-rings on the Decker saddle. Panniers need to be balanced on both sides of the saddle so that one does not significantly outweigh the other. Provisions can also be carried on the top of the pack saddle. Sleeping bags carefully rolled or placed in a pack can be fastened to the top of the saddle with rope hitching or even bungee cords. *(cited from: https://animals.mom.me/pack-mule-9165.html)*

Mules need saddles made just for mules. You may look at a mule and see similarities to a horse, but underneath the skin, their skeletal structure is fundamentally different than a horse. Using a horse saddle is going to do all sorts of damage, from causing a mule to walk funny all the way to destroying their muscles and health. A mule is also part donkey and the donkey's bone structure is fundamentally different than a horse's. The mule gets his bone structure, or skeletal structure, from the donkey. The mule's shoulder moves up and down. When you watch a mule walk, you can actually see the shoulder moving up and down. When you watch a horse walk, you'll see that they don't move up and down. The horse shoulders actually move backward and forward. When the mule walks with a horse saddle, the scapula goes up and down, continually hitting the saddle with every step. Mr Mule will not be happy with the constant impact on his shoulders. In fact, he will be in pain.

Horse   **Mule/Donkey**

The yellow lines illustrate the bars of the saddle trees which lay beneath the leather covering.

The mule is V-shaped in the shoulders, they have an hourglass belly and they carry the bulk of their weight down low. Horses, on the other hand, are A-shaped in their shoulders and they carry their weight up high. The skirting on a horse saddle is square in the front, sitting right on top of the mule's shoulder (hitting the scapula every time he takes a step). When it goes to hitting the scapula, the reverse momentum pushes it backwards so it hits the mule's hip. Double whammy!

A horse saddle has saddle bars and, rather than distributing the weight of the rider across the entirety of the back, the saddle actually creates a bridge across the back, placing the rider's weight squarely on the shoulder and the hip. On a well made mule saddle the saddle bars come up in the front by the shoulder to relieve pressure from the scapula, so it does not hit the scapula as it moves up and down. The saddle rises up in the front to accommodate the mule bone structure and movement. *(cited from: https://www.muleranch.com/mule-saddle-everything-you-need-to-know/)*

1. The seat angle on the mule saddle is a little bit deeper so that the rider's weight is not thrown forward.

2. The skirt on the mule saddle is cut back and away from the mule's shoulder. The shoulder of a mule or donkey moves up and down like a piston; a horse's shoulder moves up and forward. It's critical that the saddle not interfere with the movement of the shoulder.

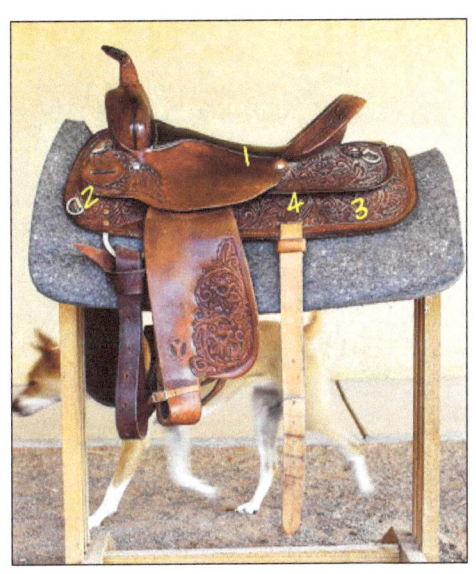

Horse Saddle

Mule/Donkey Saddle

3. A mule or donkey's back is generally shorter than a horse's back, so the saddle skirt is not as long.

4. The back cinch on a mule/donkey saddle is more important than the front cinch when it comes to keeping the saddle in place. The back cinch can be adjusted tighter than the front cinch for mules and donkeys so that it doesn't rock. *(cited from: http://www.the7msnranch.com/2011/05/mule-bars.html)*

Training A Mule

This article, by Sophia Sarember, appeared in the Spring 2000 issue of Rural Heritage. Sophia is from Tijeras, New Mexico; she gives clinics on mules, donkeys and horses (both draft and light).

Communicating with an animal is like communicating with a person who speaks a foreign language. If I am trying to get a person who speaks only Chinese to do a task for me and I speak to him in English, he will not understand. If I yell at him in English, wave my arms, and get angry he still won't understand and he may become fearful of what I am about to do. (If this sounds ridiculous, consider for a moment how some teamsters lose their tempers with their equines, which undoubtedly have perfect hearing and are quite intelligent.) In the process of getting my Chinese-speaking friend to help me in my work, I will learn a little Chinese and he will learn some English.

In trying to communicate with mules, the first thing to understand is that they want to please you. Underneath what may appear to be an unfeeling character is a willing and intelligent creature. I have had experience with draft and light horses, mules, and donkeys. I can say with confidence that after communication and trust have been established, donkeys are some of the hardest working and devoted souls I have ever dealt with. The mule inherits this quality and it makes him a reliable, dependable, and loyal fellow.

Most people who are interested in farming, driving, or riding are familiar with the horse, so their observations on the mule tend to draw comparisons to the horse. The donkey is taken into consideration as far as the mule's physical values go, yet the mule is expected to think and act like a horse. When it does not, it is labeled as stubborn or recalcitrant. Herein lies most, if not all, the difficulties that trouble mule handlers.

In addition to inheriting the donkey's penchant for hard work and loyalty, the mule acquires the donkey's attitude of extreme caution. While horses instinctively react, donkeys appear to evaluate a situation for themselves and then act. The key to working through difficult situations is directly linked to how much trust a mule has in his handler. This trust is gained through patient and systematic methods of training. Whenever a mule refuses to obey, it is because he has not understood you or he does not trust you in what you are asking of him.

You can never force a mule to obey you. If you try, any compliance will be short lived. The best methods are based on explaining to the mule what you want. If you use a method of restraint, like a twitch or a Scotch hobble, it must be approached with the idea that you are explaining to the mule that you want him to stand still, not that you are forcing him to submit.

Handlers often try to "drive" a mule to compel it to do what they wish. Horses may be driven, or pushed into an impulsive state of energy. When a whip is applied to the horse, he will instinctively spring into motion (although sometimes not in the desired direction). When a whip is applied to a donkey, his instinct is to remain where he is until he is sure of the situation. If you continue to whip the donkey, he becomes more resolute and may drop to the ground in a heap of defiance.

It is not the donkey's nature to panic and flee, as may be observed when a donkey is spooked. He will walk or trot (or, in an extremely frightening situation, canter) a short distance, stop, and evaluate conditions before going farther. A spooked horse may bolt uncontrollably over a great distance, causing harm to himself in the process. What puzzles many mule handlers is that in any given situation the mule may act like either the donkey or the horse. The muleteer must recognize and appeal to both the horse and the donkey temperament resident within the mule.

A mule's or donkey's attitude to his work is one of partnership with his handler. While well-trained horses obey without question, mules and donkeys are more task oriented. They seem to be concerned with the overall job, rather than with isolated cues. Once you have taught a job to a mule he will continue to perform the task almost unaided and in clockwork fashion. If you interfere with his task by continually giving cues, he will be offended and may resist.

Here is a simple example: I regularly ride my saddle mule Stanley through a particular gate on our property. When I return from my ride I close the gate while mounted and we go on our way. When I first taught Stanley to work the gate I had to explain with leg and hand cues how to move and what to do so I could close the gate without dismounting. Once he learned the task and knew the routine, it became his job. Now when I go through the gate Stanley automatically turns and positions himself so I may do my half of the job of closing the gate. If I were to give Stanley the physical cues to work the gate he would be confused and resentful—he knows his job, so why am I hindering him?

Some horsemen find this attribute maddening. To others it is a great asset in the process of completing daily chores. But what if you need to change your routine? That, too, is quite simple. Just explain to your mule in a quiet and confident manner that you want him to proceed on a different course.

In the example of the gate, if I no longer wanted to shut it, the first time we went through Stanley may throw his head and refuse to walk on without shutting the gate. Without reacting to his protests I would wait a moment and again ask him to go on. After a couple of days of going through the gate without closing it, he would realize that we are no longer doing this task and he would be fine. Mules can be retrained, but they need assurance that it is not their fault the retraining is required.

My mule, who happily skids logs for firewood, is also a sensitive dressage mount and jumper. Such accomplishments are within the grasp of any responsible, thinking handler. Contrary to what seems to be common belief, mules may be guided with the lightest of cues.

A mule is hard mouthed only when:

- he does not understand
- you have lost his trust
- you have pushed him past the limits of his training level

When you set out to train or retrain a mule, start at the beginning. Assuming your mule already knows something will only leave gaps in his education. Break down tasks into their simplest form, ask only for a little improvement each training session, and reward every effort your mule gives. Build successively from one training goal to another. If you are consistent, fair, and logical in your methods, your mule will gradually learn that under your apparent cool exterior lies a person who has his best interests at heart.

Whenever possible, take time to observe, read, listen, and ask questions about mules and donkeys. Your mule will be your best instructor if you take time to open a respectful dialogue.

MULE HISTORY

Under conditions of domestication it is possible to obtain hybrids between equid species. The cross that has been most significant in human history is the one between horses and donkeys to create the mule. Mules have played a key role in the development of the world. Without their hard work, stamina, strength and patience over hundreds of years prior to mechanization, much of the modern world would not exist: they helped to construct it! Through purpose driven cross-breeding, they were "designed" by man to provide the only reliable means of transport across huge expanses of land. *(cited from: http://angelajanehoward.com/the-royal-jack-and-the-knight-of-malta/)*

52 Mule Team helping build the Los Angeles aqueduct, 1912. Source: Waterandpower.org

Mules In Ancient Times

The mule has been deliberately bred by man since ancient times. The inhabitants of Paphlagonia and Nicaea (the northern and northwestern parts of modern day Turkey) are said to have been the first to breed mules.

People of ancient Ethiopia gave the mule the highest status of all the animals. The Hittites thought mules to be more valuable than a chariot horse. Sumerian texts from the third millennium BC stated the price of a mule was 20 to 30 shekels, seven times that of a donkey. The Greek writer and historian, Homer, reported in the Iliad, in 800 BC, the arrival of mules from Henetia in Asia Minor, where breeding was a specialty.

The mule was highly valued in ancient Greece as well for use as pack animals and to draw carriages. While boats were used when traveling long distances in ancient Greece, as the country was partially a group of islands, the average citizen rarely left their home area and depended upon the mule as the most common mode of transportation. Mules had much harder hooves than horses and were better suited to cover the rocky terrain found in Greece. Mules were raised in Peloponnesus and Arcadia. Harness races for mules began in Olympia in 500 BC.

Cart drawn by Mules (Koyunjik).

Detail of a mule in Assyrian sculpture, around 7th century BC. Although this particular mule is being used as a pack animal, the ancient Assyrians pioneered a communications network that saw messengers travel exclusively by mule.

A detail from a 6th century BC Caeretan hydria – a type of vase – depicting Hephaestus on a mule. One of the myths around Hephaestus involves him taking revenge against his mother, Hera, by building her a throne which she was unable to get up from once seated. Dionysus eventually went to fetch Hephaestus, got him drunk, and brought him back to Olympus on a mule. There seems to be conflicting information as to whether it was a donkey or a mule who was the sacred animal of Dionysus, but in the Hephaestus story the equine is almost always a mule.

Mules were often depicted pulling vehicles and even had their own special chariot race.

Pudes (Modest) and Podagrosus (Lame), are two of the named mules depicted on a 1st century mosaic in Ostia Antica, Italy.

In the Old Testament, the mule replaced the donkey as the "royal beast" and was ridden by King David and King Solomon at their coronations. In the kingdom of Mari in northern Mesopotamia, the story was told that the King was reprimanded and asked to "Please …use a mule instead of the common horse", as his royal position demanded. The Law of Moses (Leviticus 19:19) declared that the breeding of hybrid animals was forbidden. The Hebrews were not forbidden to use mules, but they had to purchase and import mules either from the Egyptians or the people of Togarmah (Armenia), who brought mules from the far north to Tyre for sale or barter. When the Israelites returned from their Babylonian captivity in 538 BC, they brought with them silver and gold and many animals including at least 245 mules. Two Hebrew words referring to a mule or hinny are found 17 times in the Old Testament.

Between 2100 BC and 1500 BC the Pharaohs of Egypt sent expeditions into the Sinai to mine turquoise. The miners marked their route with carvings on rocks showing boats and mules, not camels! Mules were, at that time, the preferred pack animal. While the Pharaohs were carried about in fancy litters by servants, the common people often had the use of mule drawn carts. An Egyptian monument from Thebes depicts mules yoked to a chariot. Mule remains are frequent in the archaeological record, suggesting that mules had become a "mainstream" animal early on, used primarily for pulling wagons or transporting burden.

In ancient Rome, mules were used for transport and their amazing strength and endurance was known to all.

When Hannibal crossed the Alps in 216 BC, he had mules to carry the equipment. He may even have ridden a mule in the rough terrain, where elephants could not easily maneuver.

The exact origin of the first mule though is unknown.

(cited from: https://www.columbiadailyherald.com/article/20120328/LIFE-STYLE/303289941 and https://www.mulemuseum.org/history-of-the-mule.html and http://mulography.co.uk/10-images-of-mules-in-history/)

Mules In The Middle Ages & Renaissance

Whether traveling singly, or in a group, the medieval traveler often used pack animals either to carry luggage, or to ride upon; a mule could prove its worth on medieval journeys. The mule, noted for its endurance, was an ideal mount for a long or arduous journey, particularly since it was less expensive to feed than a horse. The mules and horses who drew wagons in both the Middle Ages and the Roman Empire were, on the average, of only moderate height - about 14 hands.

The Romans had developed vast systems of stud farms to supply horses and mules for the army and for the circus. A study of original Latin sources reveals that about 50 separate breeds are defined and described. However, no large scale breeding program existed in the Middle Ages.

During the Middle Ages, horses were not classified by breed but function. It was a very simple process of classification. If you were to need a riding horse, you buy a riding horse, you need a war horse, buy a war horse. Need a cart horse? Buy a cart horse.

Courser

Types of horses were:
- **destrier**: horse of the knight, used in tournaments
- **courser:** light, fast horses, used in battle rather than the destrier
- **rouncey:** the most affordable horse and usually the animal of choice for a poorer knight or squire.
- **palfrey:** very valuable gaited riding horse that could move swiftly with great comfort for the rider
- **sumpter:** pack animal
- **hobelar:** rugged and hardy - later became known as a "hobby" horse. *(cited from: The Medieval Horse published by The Equine Heritage Institute)*

Sumpter

As early as 1294, Marco Polo reported on, and praised, the Turkoman mules he had seen in central Asia. In Medieval Europe, when larger horses were being bred to carry heavily armored knights, mules were the preferred riding animal of gentlemen and clergy.

At this point in history there was some prejudice towards the mule. The historical roots of English prejudices against mules may lay in the rejection of the Roman Catholic faith. The English associated mules with Papists and clerics during the Protestant Reformation of the sixteenth century. Much of the clergy at the time rode mules. The Victorian painting *(below)* depicts Cardinal Wolsey, in 1530, arriving on a mule at Leicester Abbey where he died. Mules were also prominent in the lands of the foes of England: France, Spain and Ireland. Additionally, the excessive demand for Irish horses to serve in England's never-ending wars pushed up prices and made mules attractive, especially for small farmers; from 1700 on, the Irish increasingly used donkeys and mules. In any event, these developments strengthened an association of mules and donkeys with Catholicism and English resistance.

Within England itself, the poor were the main employers of donkeys, and, to a lesser extent, mules. Mules were dismissed as contrary to nature, and as "polluting" mares. The portrayal of mules as "horrendous monsters" was common in English publications. Moreover, it was believed that a mare that had been mated to a jack would have donkey-like offspring when later mated with a stallion. This theory, known as telegony, went back to Aristotle. It was not until the end of the nineteenth century that scientific experiments proved that telegony had no basis in fact yet, the idea lingered on long after this scientific demonstration.
(cited from: http://animalhistorymuseum.org/ exhibitsandevents/online-gallery/gallery-8- animals-and-empire/enter-gallery-8/i-imperial-species/mules/)

Cardinal Wolsey, in 1530, arriving on a mule at Leicester Abbey

The horse defined the Middle Ages! Horses, along with mules and donkeys, were relied on for transportation, agriculture, war and recreation. A large part of the population was dedicated to occupations that used or cared for horses.

During the Middle Ages the Christian church was growing due to the missionary work of monks. Missionaries often had to travel long distances over uncertain roads. Trade routes were also very busy during the Middle Ages; the world became very interconnected. There were horses and mules used everywhere for many things. Mule trains were often used for land travel. The Catholic church was a major part of everyday life and it became the only universal European institution. It influenced all aspects of European life and encouraged people to perform astonishing acts of devotion. Among these acts of devotion to God were the pilgrimages to special holy places like the Holy Land. Pilgrimages would be like vacations today.

People of the Middle Ages wanted to see and touch places and objects that were considered holy. People could also visit holy sites to make amends for having committed sin. By doing a pilgrimage as a penance, they also hoped for the simple pleasure of traveling. A pilgrimage was an exciting, challenging opportunity to leave village life behind. For reasons of safety, pilgrims in the Middle Ages tended to do the journey in groups. *(cited from: The Medieval Horse published by The Equine Heritage Institute)*

Going on a pilgrimage in the Middle Ages was quite an ambitious and incredibly difficult journey. It required true dedication, physical and mental strength. Many of the pilgrimages were more than 3,000 miles in distance. On his frequent pilgrimages to Rome, Saint Bobone (c. 986) always took a mule with him but scarcely rode it, preferring instead to wear himself out with the effort of walking. *(cited from: Pilgrimage to Rome in the Middle Ages: Continuity and Change by Debra Julie Birch)*

The First Crusade was called by Pope Urban II in 1095 during a momentous speech in Clermont-Ferrand in France. By the middle of 1096, the main force was ready to leave and the Crusades began in earnest. Enduring the heat of an Anatolian summer and a lack of water, many Crusaders of the First Crusade dropped out along the continued march southwards. Large numbers of their horses died, leaving Crusaders riding donkeys and mules as they faced the terrifying traverse of the Taurus Mountains. *(cited from: https://www.historyfiles.co.uk/KingListsMiddEast/CanaanOutremer.htm)*

Mounted warriors often rode mules during the march leading their chargers beside them and only switched mounts before battle.

The use of pack mules was very important during the Crusades.

2 Samuel 18:9 – And Absalom rode upon a mule, and the mule went under the thick boughs of a great oak, and his head caught hold of the oak, and he was taken up between the heaven and the earth; and the mule that was under him went away. From the Crusader Bible in the Morgan Library.

Scene from an early 13th century copy of Maqamat al-Hariri

Several illustrated chronicles were created in the Old Swiss Confederacy in the 15th and 16th centuries. They were luxurious illuminated manuscripts produced for the urban elite of Bern and Lucerne and their copious detailed illustrations allow a unique insight into daily life of late medieval Switzerland on the eve of the Reformation. The most important of these chronicles are the works of the two Diebold Schillings. The magnificent illuminations below, depicting mules, are from the illustrated chronicle by Diebold Schilling of Lucerne.

Mules were used for farming, in mills and, they were the legs of "Moving and Storage" of the Middle Ages. Images of mules are found in many illuminations.

Mules Throughout Europe

When the Moors conquered Spain in the 8th century, they brought their horses and mules with them for the conquest. Mules were often used to carry the booty the Moors had blundered. They continued to systematically breed mules that were suited to the rough terrain of the area. When the Moors were driven out in the 13th century, the mules remained. Spain became a leader in mule breeding. These are the mules and jacks that started the mule industry in America 500 years later.

Monarchs in Spain however, believed that a cavalry, in order to be effective, needed to ride horses, not mules. People so preferred mules to horses that in 1248 King Alfonso issued an edict for caballeros to stop riding the preferred mules and switch to horses. King Ferdinand also issued a degree that only clergy and women could ride mules and anyone else caught riding a mule would be be-headed!

France was breeding mules in the Poitou region as long ago as the 10th century. Mule breeding began as part of a labor shortage since Europe was in constant wars. Spanish jennets and jacks were used to develop the famous Poitou jacks. The French bred for heavy draft type mules. France used large, 16 hand, 1,400 pound mares, that were a sharp contrast to the refined Arabian

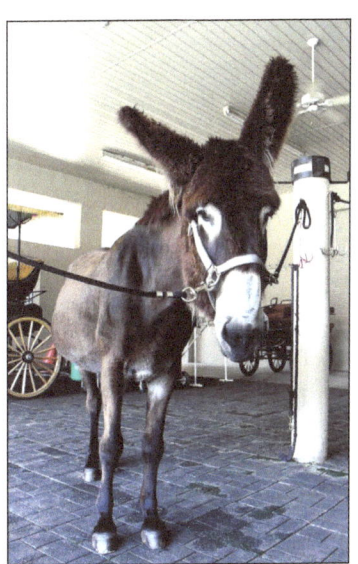 

Nicolette, a Poitou Mule, in her summer and winter coats. Gloria Austin purchased Nicolette for the Grand Oaks Resort.

horses of Spain, to breed mules. It was an immediate success and the province of Poitou became famous for the large draft mules they produced. During the 19th century, the Poitevin mares in the Poitou were almost exclusively used for the production of mules.

Breeders produced horses only when the mares could not produce mules. The most perceptive among the breeders, however, would put their mares to a Poitou draft stallion in their older years so as to conserve bloodlines. The giants among the mules were sold all over the world.

Whether driven, as a pack animal or ridden, the Poitou donkey has many qualities. Its large size is its major asset for riders and its calm nature is much appreciated. Just as for the Poitevin draft horse, its unusual looks are a real asset for the tourism industry today. Its capacities in terms of endurance and traction are absolutely on a par with other breeds of donkey. *(cited from: https://www.energie-cheval.fr/en/menu-secondaire/la-filiere/anes-mulets/races-mulassieres-du-poitou/)*

Caravan of mules transporting Spanish wine to France, illustration by Henri Valentin from L'Illustration, Journal Universel, No 612, Volume XXIV, November 18, 1854.

The British however rejected the mule while the Irish understood the value of a good mule. Those with extensive military experience could not understand the English prejudice toward the mule. It seems that the English could not adjust their equine tastes to take advantage of the talents of the mule. The sketch below shows the winners of the mule and donkey show under the patronage of the Prince of Wales and other "distinguished noblemen". The intent of the show was to improve the treatment and condition of mules and donkeys.

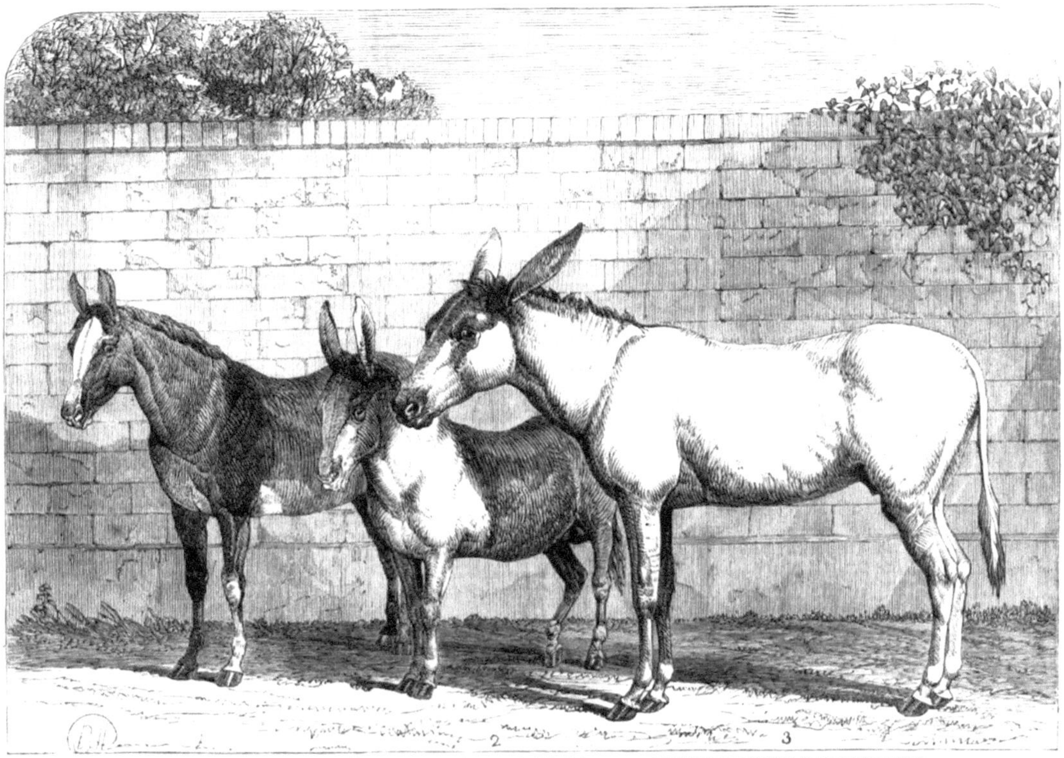

MR. D. SYKES' MULE "THE STAG." LADY V. CECIL'S DONKEY "SNOWBALL." EGYPTIAN DONKEY BELONGING TO THE PRINCE OF WALES.

PRIZE DONKEYS AND MULE AT THE SHOW IN THE AGRICULTURAL HALL, ISLINGTON.—SEE NEXT PAGE.

The Illustrated London News, volume XLIV, August 20, 1864. "The three animals represented in our Engraving, which is from a sketch by Mr. B. Hering, are as follow: No. 1, "The Stag," a mule, aged five years, belonging to Daniel sykes, Esq., of Pinner Park farm, Middlesex. No.2, "Snowball," a donkey, aged five years, belonging to Lady V. Cecil, Burghley House, Stamford. No. 3, An Egyptian donkey, presented by the Pacha of Egypt to the Prince of Wales: for the use of the infant Prince.

Mules In The New World

By the 18th century, the breeding of mules had become a flourishing industry in Spain, Italy and France. For many years the French Province of Poitou was the primary European breeding center, with some 500,000 mules bred each year. Heavier draft mules were demanded for farm work and a local breed of stud donkey became most popular. Soon, Spain was at the forefront of the mule-breeding industry as Catalonia and Andalusia each developed a larger and stronger breed of donkey. Mules were not as prevalent in Britain or America until the late 18th century. The chief demand for mules in Britain was for service in India and elsewhere abroad.

In 1495, Christopher Columbus brought four jack donkeys and two jenny donkeys to the New World, along with horses. Mule packing was important in Spain. The skill was further refined by Spanish speaking people in the New World. Natives of Latin America, especially Honduras, Mexico and southwestern areas of the United States used mules extensively for packing in early times. Columbus' purchasing agent must have had budget restrictions because his foundation jack stock was small, cheap and would have been rejected by packers in Spain. Some historians ascribe their origin to Italy while others claim Portugal as their country of origin. Regardless, these animals were instrumental in producing mules for the Conquistadors in their exploration into the American mainland. Ten years after the conquest of the Aztecs, a shipment of three jacks and twelve jennies arrived from Cuba to begin the breeding of mules in Mexico. Female mules were preferred for riding while the males were preferred as pack animals throughout the Spanish Empire. Mules were not only used in the silver mines, but were very important along the Spanish frontier. Each outpost had to breed its own supply and every hacienda or mission kept at least one stud jack. *(cited from: https://www.mulemuseum.org/history-of-the-mule.html and "The Missouri Mule: His Origin and Times p.38)*

"Coronado's March" by Frederic Remington depicts the expedition led by Francisco Vasquez de Coronado, 1539-1542.

In the early period of colonizing the New World, the mule was used for carrying silver and also for mining. The Potosi mine was the real "El Dorado" of the Spanish colonialists. 8,000,000 people died in the course of extracting its silver. Many mules also died at a horrendous rate. Walking round and round, driving the milling machine, it is said that they had a working life span of just two months and that human slaves were often brought in to replace them. The main mule suppliers to the mine were Jesuits in what is now Argentina and Paraguay. Over time indigenous people became expert breeders. There was always a link between the demand for mules and their price with the level of activity in the mines.

Besides the mines, there was also a busy regional trade in the Andes. It involved sugar, wheat, cotton and brandy. A traveler at this time with the pen name Concolocorvo talked of 50,000 to 60,000 mules used for transport in the highlands. There is some belief that there was a distinct transfer of wealth to the transportation sector making muleteers powerful and wealthy. The mule, above all else, was the "truck" that transformed transport in the region. *(cited from: Donkeys and mules in the 'New World' John Barker)*

A fanciful 1875 illustration showing the myriad of sizes and breeds of donkeys and mules.

Mules In America

In 1785, there were no mules in America—at least none on record in the new United States. In 2007, there were 28,000. But in 1925, the very peak of American "muledom", there were nearly 6 million mules in the United States, most of them in the South, most of them in harness, most of them plowing.

In the mid-1700s the best jackasses in the world were in Spain. They were animals of remarkable strength and endurance, which the monarch had long guarded by prohibiting their export.

Donkeys were already in America, as they came over with the early explorers, but they were quite small. George Washington wished to breed the very best mules, but he faced a major obstacle - the Spanish government at that time prohibited the acquisition or exportation of the famous Andalusian donkey.

After the Revolutionary War, Washington started a program to develop a larger, stronger mule to be used on farms to replace horses in the field. Washington wrote to King Charles III of Spain requesting permission to purchase good quality breeding stock. In 1785, the census for Mount Vernon listed 130 working horses and no mules. In October of 1785, a ship docked in Boston harbor carrying a gift from the King for Washington. The King sent two fine Spanish jacks and three jennies to Washington. One of the Jacks died en route and the surviving mule was named "Royal Gift" in honor of the King. To Washington's surprise, Royal Gift refused to perform his duty on the 30 plus mares awaiting his services. Undoubtedly, the exhaustive trip to a foreign land full of American mares distracted this royal gift. Fortunately, the following spring, Royal Gift responded positively to his duties and the American mule-breeding business was under way.

GENERAL WASHINGTON'S JACK ASS.

THIS is the true picture of that Celebrated Animal, which his Most Catholick Majesty the King of Spain Bought with his own money and Shipped at his own Expence, for a present to our beloved General.

Hero merit takes, and Gallant Actions thine
Or Mighty Sir, this Ass had ne'er been thine,
Though droll the Gift, yet from a King tis' good:
Asses, Kings, Ministers are all one blood.

In 1786, the Marquis de Lafayette sent Washington a black Maltese jack called "Knight of Malta", along with several jennies. These animals bred with the Andalusians, and the crossing of the Spanish and Maltese strains created highly valuable stock, known as the "compound", which was the beginning of the "American Mammoth Jackstock". In 1786, Washington advertised the "compound's" services in a Philadelphia journal. The stud fee for serving horses was a third less than it was for serving donkeys. It is said that mules from Washington's stock became the forerunners of mules that were the backbone of American agriculture for generations in the southern U.S.. *(cited from: https://www.mulemuseum.org/history-of-the-mule.html and https://www.columbiadailyherald.com/article/20120328/LIFESTYLE/303289941)*

By 1799, the year President Washington died, Mount Vernon listed 25 horses and 58 mules.

Washington's Virginia homestead of Mount Vernon would continue to flourish after his passing in 1799 up until the late 1840s. Sadly, his great-great-nephew could not pay for the upkeep of the vast estate on the Potomac's riverbank. The facilities, and preciously maintained farmland, began to decay. In 1853, a group of women, known as the Ladies of Mount Vernon, took on the task of restoring Washington's most beloved farm and home. Today the property is not only in its exact Washingtonian glory in structure and land, but also in livestock. Washington's rare beasts (including a camel), unique cattle, and yes, his mules, once again grace the estate and are on view for the public.

There are many jacks and jennies and a few mules in America which purportedly trace their lineage back to Royal Gift, America's first finely bred mammoth jack. *(cited from: https://www.horsenation.com/2012/09/10/horses-in-history-george-washingtons-mule-fetish/)*

> ROYAL GIFT, AND THE KNIGHT OF MALTA, two valuable JACK ASSES,
>
> WILL cover Mares and Jennies at MOUNT-VERNON, this Spring, for Five Guineas the Season.
>
> The first, is of the most valuable Race in the Kingdom of Spain.——The other, lately imported from Malta, by the Way of Paris, is not inferior.——ROYAL GIFT, (now 5 Years old) has increased remarkably in Size since he covered last Year—and not a Jenney, and scarcely a Mare to which he went, miss'd.——THE KNIGHT OF MALTA will be 3 Years old this Spring—is near 14 Hands high—most beautifully formed for an Ass—and extremely light, active and sprightly.——Comparatively speaking, he resembles a fine Courser.
>
> These two JACKS seem as if designed for different Purposes equally valuable.——The first, by his Weight and great Strength, to get Mules for the flow and heavy Draught.——The other, by his Activity and Sprightliness, for quicker Movements on the Road.——The Value of Mules, on account of their Longevity, Strength, Hardiness and cheap keeping, is too well known to need Description.
>
> MAGNOLIO Stands at the same Place, for FOUR POUNDS the Season.——The Money, in every Case, is to be paid at the Stable, before the Mares or Jennies are taken away.——No Accounts will be kept.——Good Pasture, well enclosed, will be provided, at Half a Dollar per Week, for the Convenience of those who incline to leave their Mares, and every reasonable Care will be taken of them; but they will not be ensured against Theft or Accidents.
>
> JOHN FAIRFAX, OVERSEER.
>
> Mount-Vernon, March 12, 1787.

By 1808, the U.S. had an estimated 855,000 mules worth an estimated $66 million. Mules were rejected by northern farmers, who used a combination of horses and oxen, but they were popular in the south where they were the preferred draft animal. One farmer with two mules could easily plow 16 acres a day. Mules not only plowed the fields, but they harvested crops and carried the crops to market. On tobacco farms, a mule-drawn planter was used to set the plants in the ground. Harvested tobacco was pulled on wooden sleds from the fields to the barns.

A COTTON PLANTATION ON THE MISSISSIPPI.

Canals were waterways through the wilderness. The Erie Canal was built to bring trade from what was the American West back to the Port of New York. Originally, it ran 363 miles from where Albany meets the Hudson River to where Buffalo meets Lake Erie. The entire canal opened in 1825 and cut transport costs into, what was then the wilderness, by about 95%. It resulted in a massive population surge in western New York, opened regions further west to increased settlement and was a prime factor in the growth of New York City as a port of trade. Canal channels were 4 to 5 feet deep and mostly mules pulled the flat bottom scows up and down the canal. Between 1825 and 1900, hundreds of thousands of mules labored on the canal towpaths.

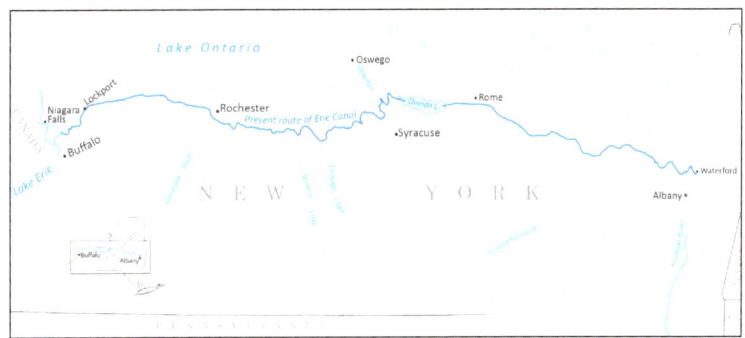

Engraving of a lock showing a packet boat in a lock and a gatekeeper preparing to close the lock gates. A team of mules and their driver wait for the boat to "lock through," while another person secures the boat to a post with rope. Published in Jacob Abbott's "Marco Paul's Voyages & Travels on the Erie Canal, 1852."

A single mule could pull 30 tons of cargo working in 6 hour shifts. The mules pulled the barges at 4 mph; they were capable of pulling the barges at 10 mph but they would wash out the banks at that speed. The shipping lines built stables all along the Erie Canal; that is how upstate New York developed. The mules were driven by hoggees; a Scottish word for "worker". Hoggees were typically young boys, 12 - 13 years old, and often they were orphans. They slept and ate with the mules and they were charged with feeding and caring for the mules. At some points on the canal the tow path was so narrow that the mule would fall off. There were ramps to get back up - and most of them made it!

Mule tenders barracks in Griggstown

By 1840, a quality jack used for mule breeding could fetch up to $5,000 in Kentucky, then a leading mule-breeding state. A large number of donkeys were subsequently imported from Spain and in the decade between 1850 and 1860 the number of mules in the country increased 100 percent. More than 150,000 mules were foaled in the year 1889 alone, and by then mules had entirely replaced horses for farm work.

In the 1840's, as settlers from the east moved west, the mule was by far the favorite pack animal. Even during the years of Spanish influence in the Southwest, when horses, burros, llamas, dogs, and even camels were used, the Mexican mule was preferred. The Mexican breed was soon replaced by the American variety; most of which came from Missouri.

Young Hoggee with his mules

Mule stable in Kingston

On the historic Old Spanish Trail that connected Santa Fe and Los Angeles, trains of pack mules were used from 1829 to 1849. High quality woolen products from New Mexico Territory were often traded for good mules. The 2,700 mile long trail was considered the longest, most crooked and difficult trail for pack mules in the history of America. The first group ever to travel over that trail consisted of 60 men and 100 mules.

On wagon trains across the plains, mules could cover 30 miles a day, while wagons drawn by horses and oxen could average only 5 miles a day. Thousands of mules were used to pull the pioneer's wagons westward, and when families found a place to settle and build their homesteads, the mules were there to haul the logs for the houses. Western explorers and trailblazers knew the benefit of choosing a good mule and taking care of it.

The San Antonio–San Diego Mail Line, also known as the Jackass Mail, was the earliest overland stagecoach and mail operation from the Eastern United States to California in operation between 1857 and 1861. It was dubbed "Jackass" because in the most severe part of the journey crossing the California desert, no stages rolled. The passengers had to ride on the "hurricane deck of a mule". The route went from San Diego, through El Paso, to San Antonio. This caused one newspaperman in northern California to declare the line went "from no place through nothing to nowhere."

Butterfield Overland Mail Company

This mail service preceded the Pony Express in the USA by eight years. It covered 900 miles in coaches pulled by mules and had just one major supply station. It was created, organized and financed by James E. Birch the head of the California Stage Company. On September 20, 1858, the Butterfield Overland Mail Company began operating their stageline over the road using the station sites pioneered by Birch and Woods from El Paso, Texas, to Warner's Ranch, California. After the final suspension of the Butterfield Overland Mail, March 12, 1861, the San Antonio and San Diego Mail Line reorganized and merged its interests under the title of the Overland Mail Corporation.

Stage coach lines also preferred mules to horses. Stage coaches were pulled by large mules that could travel six to ten miles per hour over flat, dry land. On the roughest Western roads, the Butterfield Overland Mail and later Wells, Fargo & Co., frequently transferred passengers and mail to lightweight, more durable celerity wagons or to the less expensive, but also light mud wagons.

Army Pack Mule Train by Frederic Remington

During the Indian wars in the American southwest, mules set a number of endurance records. In 1882, a company of scouts and one pack train, loaded 200 pounds on a mule and left the San Carlos agency in Arizona on a three-day march. In those three days, the mule covered 280 miles. Another pack train covered 108 miles in 16 hours while a third traveled 85 miles in desert heat in just 12 hours.

General George Crook, in the late 1870's, preferred to ride his mule "Apache", which he considered much superior to the horse, and he continually stressed the importance of having healthy pack mules under his command. He believed that the success of any campaign, to a great extent, depended upon them. General Crook's mules easily carried twice the load the Army manual stipulated because he allowed only the best equipment to be used on the best mules and each pack saddle was tailored to fit each mule. Crook's troops always had the ammunition they needed because his mule trains never failed. General Crook not only excelled in the campaigns he led, but he was also kind to his adversaries and kept every promise he ever made.

When gold was discovered at Sutter's Mill in California, pack trains soon became indispensable in hauling supplies from the port at San Francisco to the gold fields on the western Sierra slopes. By 1852, more than 16,000 mules, valued at more than $800,000, were concentrated in the northern counties. About 1,800 mules operated out of Shasta alone. By 1855, the California mule population swelled to over 31,000. A "Pack-Mule Express" business not only carried special delivery mail to the mining communities, but it also transported gold from mines to banks. Since each miner consumed at least a pound of supplies daily, packing to the mines required large numbers of mules: 2,500 mules carried freight from Marysville to Downieville, for example, providing employment for perhaps four hundred men. One thousand pack mules left Marysville in one day, carrying one hundred tons of freight, the equivalent of two steamboat loads. Packing was a seasonal business, but sometimes pack trains operated in the Sierra winter, carrying barley along with the freight because there was no forage for the animals. Sometimes animals and muleteers froze to death. Other mules perished in falls caused by shifting packs or unstable ground, and robbers and hostile Indians sometimes attacked the trains

A huge freight schooner *(right)* pulled by a six-span team of mules pauses at Webster's Station, in the shadow of Sugar Loaf Mountain on the Placerville Road, about 1865. Built along stretches of the old Johnson's Cutoff, an alternative to the Carson Emigrant Trail, the road opened in 1858, and until the decline of the Comstock Lode in the mid-1860s, it was the great artery of travel over the Sierra Nevada. In addition to the tons of freight that rumbled over the road, thousands of overland travelers passed this way, including Horace Greeley and Mark Twain. *(cited: Courtesy Society of California Pioneers)*

With the discovery of borax in Death Valley, California in the early 1890's, William Tell Coleman's company used the famous 20-mule teams to haul the product to the nearest rail junction in Mojave, California. Two 10-mule teams were hitched together to form a 100-foot long 20-mule team. Between 1883 and 1889, Coleman's teams hauled two 16-foot long wagons loaded with borax, plus a 1,200 gallon water tank (with a total weight of over 36 tons) from the Harmony Borax Works near Furnace Creek in Death Valley to Mojave; some 165 miles away! During those years, the 20-mule teams hauled over 20 million pounds of borax out of Death Valley. On those 20-day round trips, over treacherous, mostly water-less terrain in extreme high temperatures, not a single mule was lost - a tribute to the stamina of the mule. The "20-Mule Team" symbol was first used in 1891 and was registered in 1894.

Teams of 20 mules hauled two 16-foot long wagons loaded with borax, plus a 1,200 gallon water tank (with a total weight of over 36 tons)

This photo puts the size of the wagons in perspective!

Historic 20 Mule Team Borax Wagon Train as it freighted supplies out of Death Valley, in the 1880's, to the Mojave Railway.

When a young Scotsman named John Muir (April 21, 1838 - December 24, 1914) arrived in San Francisco in 1868, it is said that he asked for directions to "anywhere that's wild." He was pointed toward the Sierra Nevada, and it was there that a love story between man and nature began. Legend has it that he shouted with joy when he first saw Yosemite. Muir was not pleased to see the Yosemite he loved invaded by cattlemen, shepherds and land speculators. One summer, with his trusty mule, Brownie, he traveled extensively in the Sierra Nevada to study the threatened territory. He was exhilarated each time he encountered an alpine meadow of wildflowers, but also wondered if their kind would survive to

witness the 20th century. His arguments for preserving them included their value as watersheds for the water-dependent San Joaquin Valley agricultural industry. Muir worked ceaselessly to keep Yosemite intact and in its original state. In 1903, President Teddy Roosevelt accompanied Muir on a camping trip in the Yosemite Valley, where they slept under the stars at Glacier Point. The President later remarked that "lying out at night under those giant Sequoias was like lying in a temple built by no hand of man, a temple grander than any human architect could by any possibility build." By the time Muir met Roosevelt, he had already formed the influential Sierra Club in 1892 to secure Federal protection for the Yosemite region.. He would go on to publish six volumes of writings and pen 300 essays on preservation. Known as the "Father of the National Parks", Muir's efforts were rewarded when the U.S. Congress created the National Park Service in 1916.

In the summer of 1893 Frederic Remington visited Yellowstone, America's first national park, to research an article on its soldiers for Harper's Weekly. While there, he joined superintendent George S. Anderson and longtime government scout Felix Burgess on an expedition to the park's back county in search of animal poachers. This watercolor depicts Burgess leading a group of mounted soldiers and pack mules through a spongy mountain meadow in search of solid ground.

On the Head-Waters--Burgess Finding a Ford By Frederic Remington

Over the years, the mule and his papa, the jackass, have morphed into being portrayed in most Western TV shows and movies as coming from the Jed Clampett side of the equine family tree. The exceptions among these include Ruth, the steadfast mount of Gunsmoke's Festus, and Roscoe, ridden by Shotgun Gibbs in The Life and Legend of Wyatt Earp. But the truth is, many well-known folks in the frontier West rode mules—and liked them! *(cited from: https://truewestmagazine.com/the-history-of-mules/)*

George Custer's scouts (from left): Bill Comstock, Ed Guerrier, Thomas Adkins and Moses "California Joe" Milner—ride horses and mules in this photo probably taken in 1867 during Maj. Gen. Winfield Scott Hancock's campaign in Kansas.

In 1884, author, artist and explorer Frederick Samuel Dellenbaugh, photographed on his mule at Fort Defiance, Arizona Territory. He first visited Arizona in 1871-'73 as a 17-year-old member of Maj. John Wesley Powell's second expedition down the Colorado River.

High in the Bolivian Andes of South America, Butch Cassidy sits on his mule at far left, while the Sundance Kid fiddles with the bridle of his mule. This is reportedly the last photo taken of the two outlaws. Courtesy Robert G. McCubbin Collection.

Mules quickly replaced horses as the draft stock of choice for traders' wagons, which created a demand for mules in Missouri. Traders returning from New Mexico typically brought back mules, jacks, and jennets. One returning caravan in 1829 drove a herd of 2,000 horses, mules, and jacks across the Great Plains to Missouri. Because of their hardiness, mules became the favorite riding animals of traders and mountain men like Kit Carson, William Bent, and "Uncle Dick" Wootton.

Even cowboys in Texas rode mules!

The mule became the working brute of the U.S. Army, pulling army wagons and comprising pack trains across the West. With the Army's expanding role in the Indian Wars, along with the ever-increasing demand for draft stock by freighters on the overland trails, Missouri's mule industry exploded. Mule buyers traveled throughout Missouri, and auctions in Kansas City and St. Louis drew buyers from across the country. After the start of the Spanish-American War in 1898, the Army bought thousands of mules (at about $100 each) at the St. Louis stockyards, spending as much as $75,000 each day. By 1897, the number of mules had expanded to 2.2 million, worth $103 million. With the cotton boom, primarily in Texas, the number of mules grew to 4.1 million, worth $120 each. One-fourth of all the mules were in Texas and the stockyards at Fort Worth became the world center for buying and selling mules. By 1922, Missouri had an estimated 440,000 mules. *(Mules in America section cited from: https://www.mulemuseum.org/history-of-the-mule.html and https://www.parks.ca.gov/?page_id=25449 and https://en.wikipedia.org/wiki/San_Antonio%E2%80%93San_Diego_Mail_Line and https://truewestmagazine.com/the-jackass-mail/ and http://sweetheartsofthewest.blogspot.com/2015/09/war-hero-and-humanitarian-general.html and http://www.ohranger.com/yosemite/john-muir and https://publishing.cdlib.org/ucpressebooks/view?docId=ft758007r3&chunk.id=d0e10744&toc.id=d0e10615&brand=ucpress and https://www.americancowboy.com/people/where-did-it-come-mules and https://www.historynet.com/6-million-mules.htm)*

The mule-carts, unloading schooners anchored in the shallow waves. Galveston, TX. Illustrated by J. Wells Champney. 1975

Mule working as a photographer's assistant.

The great event cutting across the history of the American mule was the Civil War. In the war's last eight months alone, some 74,000 mules passed through the Eastern Branch Wagon Park in Washington, D.C., where Harvey Riley was superintendent. How many mules served in the war, North and South, is impossible to say, but the number probably approached half a million, most of them pulling the army's livelihood in wagons.

The Civil War introduced mules to tens of thousands of humans who had never met any of their kind before. For some—like the freed slaves who believed they would be given 40 acres and a government-surplus mule—this was a potential blessing. But for the mules it was a curse. Grant, writing about an earlier era, explains why. The soldiers who became mule drivers, he notes, "were principally foreigners who had enlisted in our large cities, and, with the exception of a chance drayman among them, it is not probable that any of the men who reported themselves as competent teamsters had ever driven a mule-team in their lives, or indeed that many had any previous experience in driving any animal whatever to harness." The result was frustration, abuse, inveterate hostility and a cancerous prejudice against mules. Harvey Riley's instructions to the new mule hand, gleaned from his experience with government mules in the Civil War: "Don't spring at him, as if he were a tiger you were in dread of. Don't yell at him; don't jerk him; don't strike him with a club, as is too often done; don't get excited at his jumping and kicking." Riley's remedy was kindness! (*cited from: https://www.historynet.com/6-million-mules.htm*)

Mules were generally used in preference to horses for wagon trains because they could more readily endure the rough roads, poor fodder and generally hard treatment. Horses were ordinarily used for artillery teams where stability and speed were more important. While horses were also preferred for ambulances, most units used the more available mules.

Mule teams were hitched to wagons in three pairs, the lead pair in front, then the swing pair, then the pole (or wheel) pair nearest to the wagon. The driver, called a mule skinner, rode the near (left) pole mule, which had a saddle, and guided the lead team with a long single rein that traveled through loops on the harness of the swing pair to the bit of the near leader, from which an iron rod led to the bit of the off (right) leader. A steady pull on the rein while shouting "Haw!" would head the team to the left; short jerks and "Gee!" would head them to the right ("Yay!" meant straight ahead.). For downhill travel, a wagon brake could be operated from the saddle.

Mule skinners were reputed to have used original and colorful vocabularies when addressing their mules, but a skinner with a good team could guide them using only his voice. Although a six-mule team was the norm, fewer mules could be, and frequently were, used depending upon the load.

Typically, twenty-five wagons were needed to supply a thousand men. Sherman used some five thousand wagons during the Atlanta campaign. His trains in one line would have strung out along sixty miles of road. The order of wagon priority on the narrow roads of the era was ammunition, then troops and artillery, and lastly quartermaster supplies.

Wagons were built and repaired and horses and mules re-shod at large wagon parks, which contained repair shops, saddlers, carpenters, harness makers, blacksmiths, wheelwrights and other craftsmen. Wagon parks could service hundreds of wagons and animals at one time.

There aren't many photos of Civil War wagon trains, especially close shots, since mules and horses would not stay still for the requisite ten seconds, as existing photos attest. *(cited from: http://clevelandcivilwarroundtable.com/articles/means/wagon_trains.htm)*

The photo below is a Union army wagon train halted and guarded from Confederate cavalry near Brandy Station, Virginia, in May 1863. The photo was take by Matthew Brady. It was in May, 1863, that one of these wagon trains safely reached Brandy Station, Virginia. Its journey had been one of imminent danger as both armies were in dire need of provisions and the capture of a wagon train was as good fortune as victory in a skirmish. To protect this train from a desperate dash of the Confederate cavalry it was "parked" on the outskirts of a forest that protected it from envious eyes and guarded by the Union lines. Mr. Brady took this photograph during this critical moment. It shows but one division of one corps. There were three divisions in each corps, and there were many corps in the army, some idea of the immense size of the trains may be gained by this view. The train succeeded in reaching its destination at a time of much need. The supply trains of the great armies numbered thousands of six-mule teams and during the march the wagon train would stretch for several miles. Filled with critical provisions such as food, clothing, medicine and munitions, the supply train was a necessary lifeline of the army. While the railroad was also vital in the rapid movement of troops and provisions, the trains were limited by the scarce routes of the era. Although trains would often move much needed ammunition rapidly near the front, it was the mule and horse that often hauled it to the exhausted troops. The equines of the conflict, too, needed adequate provisions. Generals Grant and Lee were both fond of horses, having many splendid mounts between them, and they understood that all equines required sufficient rations and good drinking water to fulfill each mission. Orders and directives were issued to the armies instructing the troops on how to provide and care for the horses and mules. Late in the war, and lacking horses and mules, generals on both sides were known to say that it was easier to replace a soldier than a horse. If cavalry was going to advance, and if wagons and artillery were going to be pulled, then the horses and mules better be healthy. Trains and railroads, supply wagons, blockade runners, and ships were all considered priority targets and prizes for the enemy, so the nation's ability to collectively employ its transportation capabilities was absolutely critical to the war effort. *(cited from: http://www.thomaslegion.net/americancivilwar/totalcivilwarhorseskilled.html)*

Be sure to read the Equine Heritage Institute book "Westward Ho" for a detailed account of staging and freighting in America.

Although the moments spent in actual combat were both intense and terrifying, most of a soldier's life was tedium. He was either marching from one spot to another or waiting in camp for the next battle to be fought. To stave off boredom, he employed many methods of amusement, one of which was singing. Nothing filled the bill quite like humor. One of the best loved comic songs in the Confederate Army was "Here's Your Mule". Several differing accounts of the origin of the song are given. The most common involves soldiers in a camp taking a clever peddler's unattended mule and hiding it. When the peddler discovers the mule missing, he goes around the camp inquiring about it. After a while, a soldier would holler "Mister, here's your mule." When the peddler went toward the call, a soldier in another part of the camp would yell the same, "Mister, here's your mule." This continued, taking the peddler all over the camp.

HERE'S YOUR MULE

A Farmer came to camp one day,
With milk and eggs to sell,
Upon a mule who oft would stray,
To where no one could tell.
The Farmer, tired of his tramp,
For hours was made the fool,
By everyone he met in camp,
With "Mister, here's your mule."

CHORUS: Come on, come on,
Come on, old man,
And don't be made a fool,
By everyone you meet in camp,
With "Mister, here's your mule."

His eggs and chickens all were gone
Before the break of day,
The "Mule" was heard of all along,
That's what the soldiers say.
And still he hunted all day long,
Alas! the witless fool,
Whil'st every man would sing the song
Of "Mister, here's your mule."

CHORUS

The soldiers ran in laughing mood,
On mischief were intent;
They lifted "Muley" on their back,
Around from tent to tent.
Thro' this hole, and that, they push'd
His head, -- And made a rule,
To shout with humorous voices all,
I say" "Mister, here's your mule!"

CHORUS

Alas! one day the mule was miss'd,
Ah! who could tell his fate?
The Farmer like a man bereft,
Search'd early and search'd late,
And as he pass'd from camp to camp
With stricken face -- the fool
Cried out to everyone he met,
Oh! "Mister, where's my Mule."

CHORUS

Missouri was well situated to take advantage of the demand for mules. It sat at the edge of the frontier where mules were needed for freighting, pioneers and the military. Missouri also bordered the cotton belt.

Missouri mule breeders bred 1,000 pound "cotton" mules from hot blooded horses but they discovered that larger mules sold for more money. In addition to good jackstock, they needed the other half of the equation - a heavier horse. In Lancaster County, Pennsylvania at the time, breeders began breeding heavy horses for Conestoga wagon freighting but their numbers remained small and mostly local to Pennsylvania. In Europe 5 draft breeds had been developed. The Percheron became America's choice with Belgians a distant second. In 1851 the Percheron, Louis Napoleon was imported to Ohio. He was sold to a breeder in Illinois in 1856. He sired hundreds of offspring; 400 of his sons were also successful breeding sires. Another imported Percheron, Normandy 351, also known as Pleasant Valley Bill, sired 60 colts per year for 18 years. Percherons then came to Missouri pulling covered wagons; their strength and size were immediately recognized and coveted! The big, Percheron mares improved Missouri's mules. The mares were docile and strong and, crossed with good jackstock, they produced mules that were easier to break and train, kicked less and required less handling skills than the hot-blood cross.

By the end of the 19th century mules from Missouri were in most states of America. They were known in the West and Northwest as freighters and packers. They were used to transport immigrants and in mines. They were found working in fields of cotton, tobacco and wheat from the East to the West. They were in the oil fields of Texas and Oklahoma, pulling plows in New York City and barges on the Erie Canal.

Nobody is quite sure when the first use of the term "Missouri Mule" occurred but mules from Missouri were well known and sought after. On May 31, 1995, Governor Mel Carnahan signed a bill designating the Missouri Mule as the official state animal.

Louis Napoleon

Normandy 351 (aka Pleasant Vally Bill)

Mules in the Modern Era

Many western towns were originally laid out with extremely wide streets to allow mule teams to turn around. Shortly after the Mormon pioneers arrived, Brigham Young directed that the streets in downtown Salt Lake City be wide enough for a wagon team to turn around without "resorting to profanity." Over the years, many of those streets have maintained their 132-foot width.

An interesting article in the November 14, 1917 issue of the Breeder's Gazette discusses the "geometry" of putting together the large hitches in order to "not become addicted to strong language" when driving the large hitches.

The relationship between the growth of cities and the rail network in the 19th century is well-established, but much less attention has been paid to the increased demand for intracity transportation that railroad expansion required. Every pound of freight that traveled on the nation's expanding railroad network required local delivery, and in most cases, horses and mules provided the moving power. In the nineteenth century, cities depended on horses for internal freight movement, public transportation, private travel and emergency services. Horses also powered machinery in mills and factories, raised and pumped water, sawed wood, drove hoisting devices, construction equipment and whims to haul loads. Horses and mules even provided power to drive ferries via paddle wheels and land vehicles via turntables geared to wheels.

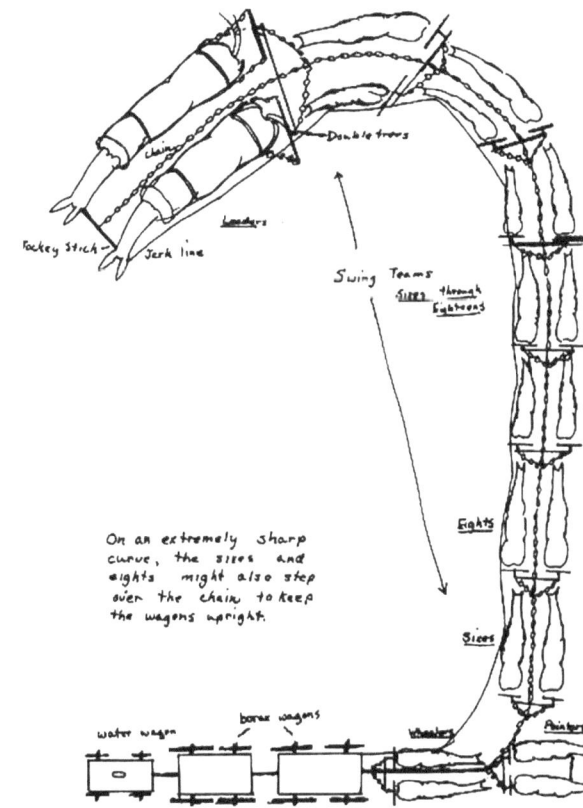

The larger wagons were driven by teamsters - largely an urban occupation. The number of teamsters grew exponentially between 1870 and 1900; the number of teamsters was growing at triple the rate that the human population grew! The teaming trades required great skill. Controlling a team was complex.

Smooth handling was vital, since abrupt starts and stops could damage freight and passengers. Moreover, poor driving could weaken, even permanently injure the legs of horses and mules.

Horses and mules also provided an important source of stationary power for construction and hoisting as well as dock and harbor work. One source estimates that in 1850, animal sources of energy in the United States provided 52.4 percent of the total work output, and of this, non-farm or urban work animals produced 2.8 billion horsepower-hours (HPH) while farm-work animals produced 2.6 billion HPH . These figures are probably underestimates and it was not until 1880 that inanimate converters in the United States surpassed the power produced by horses, oxen, and mules, both urban and non-urban.

In his 1914 book, Productive Horse Husbandry, agricultural economist Carl W. Gay entitled one of the chapters, "The Horse as a Machine," and argued that the best horses were those that produced the most work for the least food. *(cited from: : Joel A. Tarr & Clay Mcshane (2008) The Horse as an Urban Technology,Journal of Urban Technology, 15:1, 5-17, DOI: 10.1080/10630730802097765)*

Mules came to be favored over horses in the second half of the nineteenth century because they developed a reputation for hardiness and the ability to take care of themselves. In New Orleans for example, mules had the ability to endure the hot and humid climate better than horses. New Orleanians put them to work hauling garbage trucks, pulling streetcars, and even towing the Mardi Gras parade floats.

Hauling logs for lumber

Mail delivery in Tennessee

Fire hose wagon in Florida

Rapid transit in Georgia

Garbage cart in Tennessee

Delivery wagon

Mules were used to string wires from the back of a wagon for telephone service in St. Louis.

School Bus

Towing a broken down car

At the outbreak of World War I Germany had 4 million horses and mules. England and France together could only muster 6 million, but America had 25 million. Mules were the unsung heroes of World War I. According to Brigadier-General T.R.F. Bate, British Remount Commission, "Great as has been the success of the American gun horse, still greater, though perhaps less appreciated, have been the war qualities of the American mule... probably the most serviceable and satisfactory animal used in the war."

Nearly all of the British Remount purchase centers were in the United States. Mules were purchased via dealers in Missouri and Kansas and later, in the south in Tennessee, Texas, Alabama, and Georgia. Nearly all the mules used by the British came from the United States (hundreds of thousands). Italy bought U.S. mules for use as pack animals in their mountain terrain. U.S. mules also went to Egypt to serve with British troops there. Once the United States entered the war there was even more need for mules. There were 52,137 draft mules and 9,240 pack mules used by the American Expeditionary Forces in Europe, but not all of them came from the U.S.. Nine thousand were from France, 16,600 came from Spain, and 6,800 came from England. The latter, however, might well have come originally from the U.S.

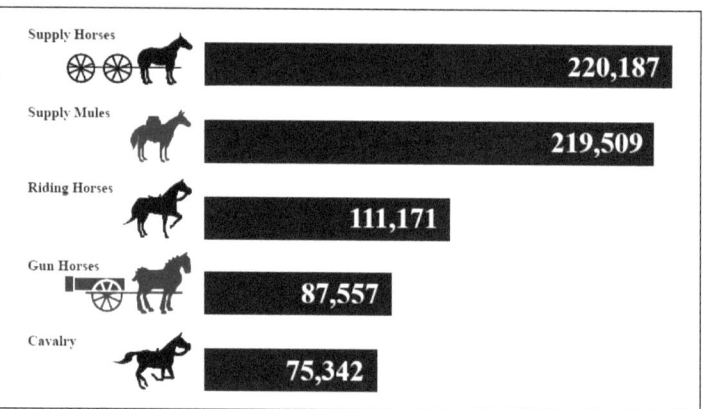

British Army in November 1918, Horses and Mules

The British requirement for mules stated that pack mules were to "have short backs, stand well, and be good boned" with weight proportional to height and conformation, weighing between 800 and 900 pounds and standing 14 to 14.3 hands barefooted. Draft mules were to be taller, 15.1 in their bare feet, and should weigh 1000 pounds. It was specifically noted that light gray or white mules were the only ones that would not be considered for purchase since they would be more visible to the enemy. *(cited from: https://www.worldwar1centennial.org/index.php/the-animals/3231-test-article-for-mules.html)*

This was a typical scene at Lathrop, Mo., when that town was a principal center of the farflung horse and mule business of Guyton & Harrington. This picture is from a book on "the world's greatest horse and mule properties," compiled in 1914 for the British government, then the firm's largest customer.

Mules gained a reputation for intelligence, for not having any patience with incompetent handlers and for an unerring instinct for self-preservation. Trucks became less reliable the closer they got to the front. The vehicles were prone to breakdowns and they were difficult to navigate on muddy roads in forward areas. Mules however, could easily maneuver on the war torn landscape of the Western Front. Strong and agile, they carried heavy loads for long distances and their surefootedness was legendary. Animals, just like soldiers, endured harsh conditions during wartime, but mules recovered from intense exertions quickly and could even subsist on vegetation when grain and hay was not available. Troops in the trenches received most of their supplies, including the all-important hot meals, by mules. Even tanks, one of the most recognizable symbols of modern warfare, depended on mules for their ammunition and gasoline. *(cited from: https://missourioverthere.org/explore/articles/missouri-horses-and-mules/)*

Be sure to read the Equine Heritage Institute book "Unsung Heroes of World War One: How Horses, Donkeys and Mules Changed the First World War" for a detailed account of horses and mules in World War I.

Every Horse and Mule With U. S. Troops Soon To Wear Nice Gas Mask

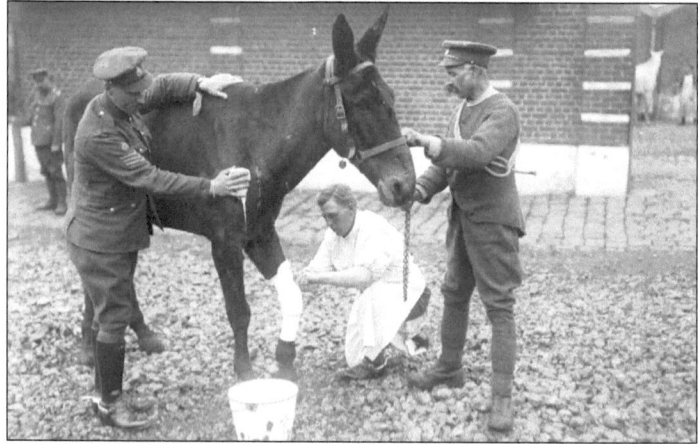

Thousands of horses and mules battling with the allied armies are being protected from the deadly German gases which have taken as heavy toll among them as among the soldiers against whom they are loosed.

Quantity production of "horse gas masks" has now been attained in this country, it was announced today, and "within a short time" every horse connected with the overseas forces will be equipped.

The U.S. Army used thousands of mules during World War II as well. In the words of a veteran of the China-Burma-India (CBI) Theater, retired Technical Sergeant Edward Rock Jr., [they] "served without a word of complaint or lack of courage. They transported artillery, ammunition, food, and medicine and, under enemy fire, transported the wounded. Many of the CBI veterans are here today because a mule stopped a bullet or a piece of shrapnel meant for the GI. Mules fell in battle, mortally wounded...and we shed tears for them."

The war was not limited to terrain accessible by motorized transport. When it came down to it, the mule was akin to a piece of equipment, like a 2 1/2-ton truck, needed to take supplies into places no truck or even jeep could go. The hardy pack animals were vital to the troops fighting in the jungles of Asia and the mountains of Italy and the soldiers loved them, particularly the mule skinners, those soldiers trained to use and care for the animals.

The most famous American unit of the CBI was the 5307th Composite Unit, also known as "Merrill's Marauders". Six Quartermaster pack troops were part of the unit, and mules were liberally issued to the rest of the unit as well to transport their own equipment and supplies. Each troop had about 300 mules and 75 men. It took four mules to carry a heavy machine gun or mortar, one for the weapon itself and the other three for ammunition. "Snuffy" was a very large creature yet very gentle to work with. His packsaddle was so heavy and he was so large that it took two men to place it on him. Robert W. Mitchell of the Orange Combat Team of Merrill's Marauders writes of his Snuffy: " Snuffy approached a sharp left turn and then disappeared into the jungle. His feet were close together, his ears pointed downhill and he sort of leaned to the left and with a side paddle made the turn, skidded the rest of the way. If a mule could talk, it is certain he would have said, 'whew!'"

When the fighting in Burma ended, the mules and horses that had served there were ordered disposed of. Some were sick after their service in the fetid jungles of Southeast Asia and had to be destroyed. A farewell volley was fired for them. Others were sent to remount stations and shipped to Eastern Europe and the Balkans as part of the Lend-Lease Program. Others were sent to farms in the Philippines or China. More still went to the Chinese Army. *(cited from: https://warfarehistorynetwork.com/2016/01/29/army-mules-the-beast-of-burden-in-war/ and http://www.chindit.net/Mules.html)*

Mules and their handlers crossing a Burmese river

Merrill's Marauders in Burma

The mountainous terrain of Italy also required the mule's services. An infantry regiment needed 250 animals per day to keep it supplied. Montecassino, Italy 1944

In 1950, North Korea invaded South Korea and the U.S. Army and United Nations Police Force fought the North Koreans and their allies, the Chinese Communists, until a cease fire in 1953. Despite knowing the necessity of mule power in guerrilla type warfare, the U. S. Army sent no mules to Korea in this conflict although the mountainous terrain resembled the mountains of Greece, Italy and Sicily. However, the North Koreans and Chinese communists did use mules and Mongolian ponies to transport supplies to their troops in the front lines. American soldiers, recognizing the value of pack mules and their need for them, captured enemy mules whenever possible. All mules captured from the North Koreans and the Communist Chinese were considered prized possessions and were carefully cared for by American soldiers liberating them.

In the spring of 1951, when the Communists mounted their offensive north of Seoul, the Army 7th regiment, 1st U. S. Cavalry pushed forward with their counterattack. As the Communists were forced back, they abandoned their animals and the U. S. Cavalry troops captured these animals. The thin and sickly mules and horses (Mongolian ponies) were quickly restored to health with better feed, including the cereal packets from the soldiers own 5 in 1 Small Detachment Rations, fed to them by the soldiers.

Even though the Army realized the unique value of mules, the decision had been made to deactivate the mules and horses section. By the end of the Korean War, the remaining mules were in 2 units at Fort Carson, Colorado, the 4th Field Artillery Battalion (pack). In 1956, the 322 remaining mules of the 2 units were sold or transferred to other agencies including the National Park Service and the Forest Service. Yosemite National Park received 30 of these well trained Army mules. *(cited from: https://www.mulemuseum.org/u-s-army-mules.html)*

One of the mules captured from Communist forces in Korea was found to have a standard U.S. Army brand (called a Preston Brand), number 08K0. When that brand was located in Army records with the mule's history, it was found that he had been dispatched to the Chine-Burma-India theater during World War II, possibly with the Mars Task Force. At the conclusion of WW II, he was transferred to the Nationalist Chinese Army. The mule must have been later captured by the Communist Chinese, then moved to the fight in Korea, finally ending up back in the hands of the U.S. Army after more than six years. He had his picture taken, then dutifully went back to work on a pack train.

Afghanistan has a rugged mountain terrain that is among the most forbidding and remote landscapes anywhere in the world. Afghanistan offers low deserts and rugged mountain ranges with high-altitude cold. That means changing the training troops receive. Afghanistan's high altitude can have a withering effect on even the most fit soldier. Heavy loads, like packs of 70 pounds or more, can be extremely difficult to carry. ENTER THE MULES. In a place as demanding as Afghanistan, the military must look at "sustainment" – the resupply, care, and feeding of the force – in a new way. The result: mule school. At the Marine Corps's Mountain Warfare Training Center, where marines and other troops are schooled in sniping, navigation, packing an animal and survival. The Animal Packing Course is a two-week program in which students learn the fine points of mule packing. The instructors take care to give students an appreciation for each of the animals. Animal packing has been used since the days of Genghis Khan and Alexander the Great and it is a skill outlined in the Marine Corps's Small Wars Manual, its tactical bible. *(cited from: https://www.csmonitor.com/USA/Military/2009/0504/p22s01-usmi.html)*

Lance Cpl. Tyler Langford, anti-tank missile-man, 3rd Battalion, 3rd Marine Regiment, leads his pack mule during a hike at Marine Corps Mountain Warfare Training Center Bridgeport, California, *(cited from: https://nationalserviceanimalsmonument.org/mules/)*

Special Forces soldiers with the 3rd Special Forces Group pictured with a mule carrying a MK-47 40mm grenade launcher as a pack load. Select Green Berets undergo the Special Operations Animal Packing Course (SOAP-C) at Fort Bragg.*(cited from: https://www.americanspecialops.com/photos/special-forces/special-forces-donkey.php)*

MULE STORIES

Sir Gawain and the Bridleless Mule

A 13th century compilation by Austrian poet, Heinrich von dem Türlin, tells how the dying king of Serre left his kingdom to his two daughters – bequeathing them a magical bridle that would preserve the kingdom for its possessor. The elder daughter, Amurfina, took both kingdom and bridle; and younger sister Sgoidamur, riding upon a bridleless mule, made her way to the court of King Arthur to ask for help. The first knight Sgoidamur meets is Kay. He takes the mule and embarks on a great journey across a deep valley full of reptiles and wide, sunny plains and dark forests full of great and savage cats who all bow before the mule. He then encounters a deep black river, wide and fast-flowing, with a bridge no wider than a hands-breadth the only way to cross it. The mule immediately jumps upon this narrow bridge and Kay returns in terror to Arthur's court.

Gawain then sets out with the mule and is courageous enough to cross the bridge. On the other side of the river he finds a curious castle – there are heads mounted on sticks outside and the high walls revolve like a millstone; meaning that Gawain and the mule only have a limited period of time to pass through the entrance on each revolution. They make it through, but the mule loses its tail.

Inside the castle is deserted, but presently Gawain meets Gansguoter – magician, builder of the castle, uncle of the two princesses and slayer of many knights. Gawain must pass several tests before he is allowed to take the bridle: first he must behead Gansguoter (who returns again the next day), then Gawain must defeat two lions, then he must defeat the knight whose previous kills are displayed on the stakes outside the castle and finally he must fight and kill two dragons. Triumphant, Gawain returns to Camelot with the mule and the bridle. All the beasts of the forest bow to both knight and mule as they pass. *(cited from: http://mulography.co.uk/four-mules-in-mythology/)*

Mule Bombs of Valverde

Texans had long claimed much of New Mexico as their own. No longer constrained by the Compromise of 1850, Confederate Texans invaded the southeastern corner of that territory in July of 1861. More Confederate forces joined them over the ensuing six months. In February 1862, Confederate Brigadier General Henry Hopkins Sibley led the 2500 men of his "Army of New Mexico" in a full-fledged effort to overrun the rest of the territory, reach the gold fields of Colorado and establish a Confederate bastion in the Far West. He was opposed by regular U.S. Army troops and regional volunteers of the Department of New Mexico, under the command of Colonel E.R.S. Canby. By February 20th, Sibley was encamped behind the Mesa del Contadoro, on the east side of the Rio Grande across the river from Canby's headquarters at Fort Craig. After a skirmish during the day, the mostly Texan soldiers settled down for a peaceful evening in a waterless camp. Little did they know that the night would produce one of the strangest stories of the Civil War. That night, Captain James "Paddy" Graydon decided to initiate a raid on the Confederates.

Lithograph from the April 9, 1863 edition of Harper's Weekly.

There are no pictures of Paddy Graydon's Spy Company, after all...they were undercover spies! This lithograph from the April 9, 1863 edition of Harper's Weekly shows Union scouts in the southwest and gives a good picture of a scout team at work. Notice in the two bottom corners, they have taken two sentries as prisoners. Graydon's men would have also been down in the encampment, standing around the fires listening. The tools of the trade have changed over the centuries but the mission and tactics of the military scout have changed little. The primary rule - Don't get caught! Captain Graydon, was an Army captain in Arizona. He earned a reputation for his ability to spy and track Indians, Army deserters and outlaws. In 1861 he was commissioned by Territorial Governor Henry Connelly to form an Independent Spy Company. On the night of February 20th, 1862 he took two of his oldest mules and lashed wooden boxes containing howitzer shells to their backs. Graydon and a few of his men crossed the Rio Grande and stealthily led their mules close to the enemy camp, within about 150 yards of their pickets.

The raiders lit the fuses on the explosives and started the mules on their way into the Confederate lines. Unfortunately, the animals proved to be too faithful. As the soldiers withdrew, they noticed quickly and with much consternation that the mules, instead of cooperating in the destruction of the enemy force, were following them! The withdrawal became more precipitous as Graydon and his men scrambled to outdistance their faithful followers, who shortly began to explode. The Confederate camp was alarmed and went to full alert and 200 of their horses and mules panicked and dashed to the river, where they were captured. The Union soldiers returned to Fort Craig unharmed. The day after the raid Canby and Sibley's forces fought the Battle of Valverde. The Confederates achieved a tactical victory but at considerable logistical cost. Losing so many horses and mules in the stampede following Graydon's raid contributed to Sibley burning some of his own wagons early on February 21st. New Mexico militia destroyed other immobilized Confederate wagons late that day. Then five weeks later, the Battle of Glorietta Pass on March 26-28 Confederates held the ground, but the Northern troops burned most of the remaining supply trains. Since Sibley could not capture either of the primary Federal posts and depots at Fort Craig or Fort Union, he was eventually forced to retreat back to Texas with a starving and bedraggled force. Though Graydon's raid had not destroyed his foe, the loss of the horses and mules had begun the process that reduced Confederate mobility and logistical capability, eventually leading to their defeat in the campaign.

While this saga of the mule bombs was reported by Mark Twain and in the postwar *Battles and Leaders of the Civil War*, historical evidence for it is sketchy at best. But the exploit is very much in keeping with Graydon's independent and impulsive reputation. He died later that year after being fatally wounded in a gunfight over accusations he had massacred Indians. *(cited from: https://www.army.mil/article/16624/ mule_bombs_at_valverde and http://exploringoffthebeatenpath.com/ Battlefields/ForgottenFront/index.html)*

A detailed look at the American Civil War with articles originally published as "The Century War Series" in "The Century Magazine" 1887. Edited by Johnson, Robert Underwood, Clarence Clough Buel.

Smokey Joe

I have a mule: his name is Smokey Joe and he's a klutz. He's very surefooted when he wants to be — "wants" is the key word. Yes, he can climb mountains, navigate narrow trails and rock hop without taking a wrong step or missing a beat but, on flat ground, he trips over his own four feet. See, he has an insatiable appetite. I really should have named him "Hoover": not after the president, after the vacuum.

His whole goal in life is to eat as much as possible as long as possible. He's constantly looking for grass on the trail (which is few and far between out here in the desert). If he's not looking for something to eat, he's daydreaming about eating and not looking where he's going. He's fallen flat on his face a couple times with me from not paying attention on a flat, wide trail. But, take him over a cliff and it's like riding a mountain goat. This past weekend as we're hopping off a rock, he spots a sprig of grass on the way down and halfway through flight, slam dunks the grass straight into his mouth before landing.

When I'm riding and reach into my saddle bags for a water or snack he stops and turns his head wanting a bite. (Okay, maybe he's a little spoiled). Most horses and mules are afraid of things that crackle and crinkle -like plastic water bottles, plastic bags and wrappers. Not Smokey — that could be the noise of something edible. Heading home from our camp spot once, I pulled our big living quarters trailer into the gas station so I could fuel up on coffee. I made sure both mules were okay in the back of the trailer. I headed in for my liquid caffeine fix and on the way out I saw my boyfriend standing outside the trailer with the mules.

I ran over asking "are they okay? Are they colicking?" Terry replied back "I went into the trailer to get an iced tea and all of a sudden I hear this thud and some grunting. I ran out and saw that Smokey Joe had fallen and slid under Betty Boop [our other mule]. I unloaded her to get him up and out. Maybe he had a seizure… why else would he fall like that?" I looked at Smokey and he looked totally fine, like nothing had happened. I knew exactly what happened though: he dropped some hay out of his manger and put his head down to get it and lost his balance. Of course that's what it was, because he's fallen in the trailer before for the same exact reason. And if he was really shaken up by his fall, he'd be reluctant to get back in, but he basically pulled me and himself right back in because he had some unfinished business to attend to… his hay! *(cited from: Maria Wachter in Horse Nation https://www.horsenation.com/2017/11/15/smokey-joe-the-clumsiest-surefooted-mule-in-the-world/*

Zhang Guolao and His Mule

Zhang Guolao was one of the Eight Immortals – a group of legendary xian in Chinese mythology (xian means an enlightened person, someone who is spiritually and / or physically immortal). They are believed to know the secrets of nature and each represents male, female, the old, the young, the rich, the noble, the poor and the humble Chinese.

Old Age, Zhang Guolao, is one of the Immortals who actually existed as an historical figure somewhere in the seventh or eighth century. He is often depicted on his mule, with whom he could cover as much as 300 miles in one day. When he was done, he could just fold his mule up and put it in his pocket or inside a gourd. To regain the mule's true form, all he had to do was sprinkle water on it. Another story suggests that it was wine which caused the mule to change form; an unnamed emperor once rewarded the mule with wine after it performed a wonderful back-up and it promptly turned into paper.

One legend says how Zhang Gulao and his mule came across a cauldron of stew cooking in an abandoned monastery. They both devoured it only to discover that it was in fact a rare immortality potion being brewed by a local – so both Zhang Gulao, and his mule, are divine. Another origin story claims that the mule was already immortal and that Zhang Gulao claimed his own immortality by finding this mule and then using it to chase a unicorn through the cosmos. *(cited from: http://mulography.co.uk/four-mules-in-mythology/)*

Duldul

Duldul, the "first mule seen in Islam", was Muhammad's favorite. He rode her into many battles and she was of great help to him – she could sit or lie down on command. One local legend even describes how she carried the prophet up a sheer cliff to escape danger. She outlived Muhammad and was looked after by his son-in-law, who would hand feed her as by then she was old and toothless. *(cited from: http://mulography.co.uk/four-mules-in-mythology/)*

When a horse lover opens her heart to mules

submitted by: Nikki Stewart, Robbinsonville, NC

My love for equines started at a very young age. By the time I was 4/5 yrs old I was riding by myself. My Papaw had a team of Belgian horses that pulled a wagon. I thought they were the most beautiful animals I'd ever seen! He eventually sold those horses and bought a team of mules. I can remember thinking, "Why would someone want to do that?" My Papaw loved working his horses and mules and had a few different teams. He told me a story one time of a mule his Daddy had when he was growing up. This mule was one of the finest plow mules. It would work all day and do fine; maybe even a few days and no trouble. Then out of the blue it would run off. He thought his Daddy just couldn't hold it. So one day he tried plowing with the mule and yep, off he ran. He couldn't hold him either. A friend of theirs kept bugging them to selling them the mule. My Papaw's Daddy tried to tell him it would runaway when it took a notion to, but the friend kept asking and he finally sold it to him. He must've thought he could hold him. Well, the friend did fine for awhile then one day the mule ran off on the friend too!!! Haha.

Jeter the Mule. Photos by Madison Waldroup of Madison Victoria Photography

I recently got into mules and have a coming three yr old. I am learning you can't "make" them do anything they don't want to do. Even with all that, I am beginning to understand why this hybrid vigor has converted long time horse owners into mule lovers. I once heard something in the movie "Scudda-hoo Scudda-hey", it's a good old time movie highly recommended. Here are some quotes from it:

"I believe mules are special animals, they can be very humble and loyal in the right hands."
"Due to their inability to reproduce, they don't have a legacy to pass on."
"Other creatures pass this legacy on to their offspring but not Mr. Mule."
"The only legacy the mule can pass on is their loyalty to their masters…a life of hard work."
"I think this contributes to their humble personalities and part of what makes them special creatures."
"There's nothing better than a good mule, but at the same time there's nothing worse than a bad one."

Training mules is a lot different than horses. I have found out they care a lot more about their noses than their mouth. They do not like their nose to be uncomfortable. Training seems to be similar as with horses in such as ask, tell, demand, but pressure on the nose is what gets you the answer you're looking for. There is no room for mistakes by the handler. Mr. Mule is always right in his thinking and you have to teach him what you want him to do by making the wrong answer hard and the right answer easy. They sure don't forget anything! Let them get away with something and they will try it again. Consistency is extremely important while training. Mules act on their self preservation instincts. You can actually see a mule think. A horse will react when scared but Mr. Mule weighs out his options. He won't put himself in harm's way. My favorite mule trainers to watch are Steve Edwards and Ty Evans. So if you are interested in mules you might find some good info there as well..

My main reason for purchasing a mule was for their sure-footedness. A few years ago my friend Kayla Adams and I went to Cataloochee Horse camp (North Carolina) to get away for a few days. We love to ride pig trails/mountainous terrain because we get bored on the forest service roads. We left out on a twenty-five mile trek and about 1/3 of the way through, the terrain became steep and narrow on one side. One place in particular had a large rock we had to step up onto to continue moving up the mountain. My horse slipped and in the process of trying to gain footing, his hind end fell off the trail and he slid down the mountain! Of course I bailed before he went over! All I could do was stand there in terror watching him slide. About 50 yards down he slammed to a stop on a large boulder. It was very rocky where he went down and a complete miracle he didn't break anything. Even more so, it was a miracle I got him back onto the road! God was sure looking out for me that day. Kayla and I got back onto the trail and I specifically remember her saying, "Can we just thank God for a minute!" After that accident, I started to think more about getting a mule and finally took the plunge. I have to say I love my long eared friend and would have to agree that they are special creatures!

Jeter and Nikki

Jeter taking a snack break.

Roy the Big Red Mule

submitted by: M. Ryan Rose

All my life I heard about a big red mule named Roy. Roy has long since passed away and is very much missed by my family. I never met this animal, though I surely wish I would have. My Great Grandfather bought Roy and two other mules as colts. He told my Grandfather and my Uncle to break them, so they set into jumping beside them, line driving them, walking them with weight on their back, etc. When it came time to ride the mules, the first mule was saddled and threw a single buck and then settled down. The second one didn't buck but was definitely nervy and then it came time to ride Roy. Roy stood absolutely still, my Grandfather climbed atop that great animal and sat there. He merely clucked his tongue and Roy began walking. They rode him frequently, then one day a man by the name of Sam Bailey came by and saw the three colts. He like them and bought them right up. My Grandfather begged his Daddy not to sell Roy because he was so precious. Roy was sold anyway and Sam Bailey left with Roy that day.

**Example of a team of Mules skidding logs.
Sherman Myers, Cades Cove, TN - Circa 1920**

The next spring Roy came back through a very long and extensive trade. Sam Bailey had broken Roy to work and boy would he work. Roy plowed our garden a time or two before it was time for him to be logged. My Grandfather logged him for two weeks. He was calm as he could be, never gave any trouble. Whenever they hooked him to a log, it was time to watch out! He'd break belly bands when he jumped into the pull, he was so fast and strong. He'd give you ever inch and every pound of his body into a pull and then when you hollered, "Whoa", it was like locking up brakes. On the Wednesday of the third week Roy was logging, he started over a little hill and a pole he was hooked to slid up his back and pinned him to the ground. My Grandfather ran up to him and his Daddy hollered, "What do we do now?" My Grandfather said, "Daddy, we'll just cut it off." He ran over to their old dozer. He grabbed his chainsaw out of it and walked over to Roy. He didn't show Roy the saw. He pulled the chord and threw it into the log. When the log finally cut, Roy stood up like nothing happened. A chainsaw thrown wide open into a white oak pole couldn't scare that mule, I think I'd lose my mind if that happened behind me.

Mule Days

California

On Memorial Day week each year, for nearly fifty years, tens of thousands of people from all over the world have descended on the Eastern Sierra community of Bishop, California for the fun, friendship and camaraderie discovered in celebrating the resilient, tough, hardworking and friendly animal - the Mule. The celebration is called Mule Days. And of course there is an all-mule parade - no motorized vehicles allowed. In 1974 Ronald Reagan was the Grand Marshall of the parade!

It is part mule show, part test of skills, and part Wild West show. The fourteen mule shows consist of: Western, youth, English, cattle working, gaited, coon jumping, racing, musical tires, gymkhana, packing, shoeing, chariot racing, team roping and driving. Mule people are determined to prove that anything a good horse can do, a good mule can do better. From trail riding to show classes, mules can do it all with the grace unique to these animals. Steer roping and stopping, an event normally reserved for quarter horses, is another highlight of Mule Days. Cowboys will have the opportunity to prove their roping and riding skills astride some of the best working mules in the United States. *(cited from: https://muledays.org/)*

Tennessee

"Mule Day" has been a popular tradition in Columbia, Tennessee for nearly 170 years, since the 1840s. It began as "Breeder's Day", a single day livestock show and mule market event held on the first Monday in April. Over time, "Mule Day" evolved from a single day event into a multi-day festival, attracting thousands of attendees, lasting almost a week. The heavy involvement of Maury County in the mule industry has caused the event to grow over time into "one of the largest livestock markets in the world."

Events include a mule-driving contest, "working mule", and "best of breed" competitions. The annual mule pull contest requires a pair of mules to pull a sled loaded with cinder blocks 10 feet. Each pair is given 3 tries to make it the full 10 feet. The team that pulls the most weight wins. Since 1934, the festival has been highlighted by a "Mule Day Parade" including a contest for the Mule Day Queen. *(cited from: http://muleday.com/about/)*

The Great American Horse Race of 1976

The year was 1976. "People were looking for a party," recalls Curt Lewis, who in 1976 had just finished his journalism degree at Wichita State. "Vietnam was just over in '75. Watergate was over. Nixon was gone," he says. "Everyone was looking for a good time." And there was an excuse to celebrate. The U.S. was turning 200 — and the birthday party seemed to last all year. In honor of the bicentennial, trains and airplanes were painted red, white and blue. A fleet of tall ships sailed down the Hudson River. And there was a horse race unlike any other. The Great American Horse Race

It was called the Great American Horse Race, and it would span nearly 100 days and 3,500 miles, starting in New York, heading to Missouri, and then following the Pony Express route to California. Lewis was hired by the race organizers to document all the greatness and Americaness of the Great American Horse Race. And also the competition. The rider who covered the distance fastest would get $25,000 – worth about $100,000 in today's dollars.

About 100 riders signed up. Cowboys took a break from rodeos. World War II veterans, finished with their missions on submarines and B-17 bombers, also entered. So did a sheriff — and even an Austrian count. "Count Johannas Hoyos — and he was a good guy," Lewis says. And then there was Virl Norton. He was one of the oldest riders. He didn't have as big a bank account as most of the others. He didn't have any fancy horse equipment. Or a big crew to help him set up camp or cook or do laundry. But he had a plan.

While some riders entered Icelandic ponies, quarter horses, and Appaloosas, the consensus was that the horse to ride if you wanted to win was an Arabian. "The sport of endurance horse riding is won by Arabian horses," Lewis says. "The motto: if you're not riding an Arabian, you're following an Arabian." But Virl Norton was going to challenge that motto. It was the Great American Horse Race, but Virl Norton entered...a mule.

"He always had a hankering for mules, I think maybe from his childhood," says Virl's son, Pierce. Most of the riders had a crew of two or three to help along the race. Virl only had Pierce. And Pierce was only 16. "I had just gotten my driver's license in March," Pierce says. "Guess I had to learn how to drive pretty fast." Even with a mule and a crew of one teenager, Virl Norton was confident that he was going to win. "He was quite a social, charismatic guy, and we'd go into a restaurant, and he'd start talking about it," Pierce says. "And he wouldn't kind of hold back his confidence. And I would kinda' be a little sheepish back there, thinking, 'Well, we need to see what's gonna happen here." So why did Virl Norton have such confidence in his mule and his 16-year-old son?

Virl Norton was born in Wyoming in 1916. As a teenager, he caught and trained wild horses. He and his family also worked mules on their farm. "So, he had an understanding of what the strengths and weaknesses of mules were," Pierce says. Virl learned that mules are slow — generally not a good quality for a race. But he also learned that mules have stamina and durability — good qualities for the 3,500-mile Great American Horse Race.

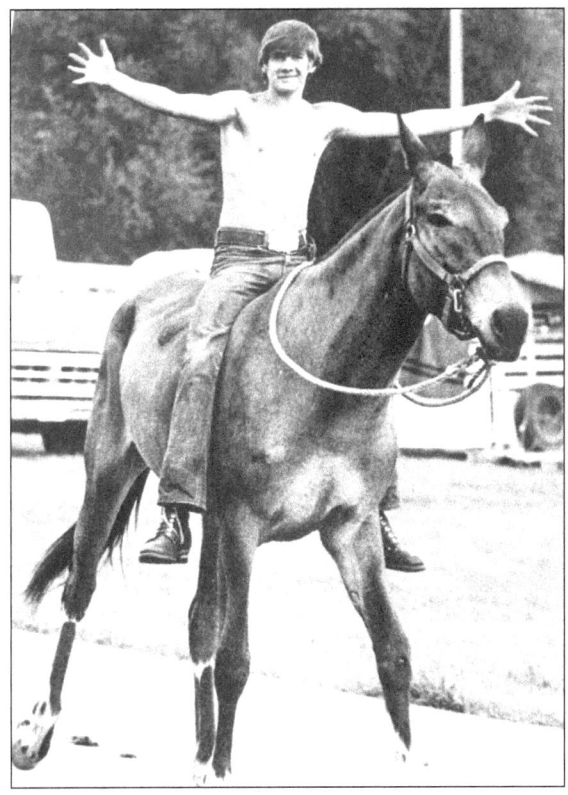

Pierce Norton was only 16 at the time of the Great American Horse Race. (Courtesy of Curt Lewis)

Virl got married and settled in San Jose, California. He worked as a steeplejack -- he went around the country painting tall things like towers and smokestacks. And he had a family. "There was five of us children and my mother," Pierce says. "And then my dad would be out painting. And he'd be out in Sacramento or North Dakota or some place, and he'd come home every couple weeks. When I was about 8 years old, my mom got breast cancer and got pretty ill. And all of us kids, since my father wasn't there all the time, we got shipped off to some relatives in Idaho and Wyoming. We were all with different relatives. "Pierce ended up in Idaho. "I went up to my uncle Delos's, who had a cattle ranch and farm," Pierce says. "And he had six kids there himself in a two-bedroom house. You're getting up in the morning, feeding cows and things like that. It's a completely different life. When I first went up there, I think kind of the pretense was, 'This is a temporary thing. We're going to go up until my mother gets better.' Now, that's what I understood as an 8-year-old kid. So I was at my Uncle Delos's house and he got a phone call. This was in the May of '69, when my mother died — and that was the phone call.

And I think I became an adult right there. Everything became clear. I'm on my own at this point." Pierce and his siblings stayed on with relatives. Meantime, Virl sold the family's home in San Jose to pay off hospital bills. He moved into a house trailer on the family ranch outside of town. But unlike his siblings, Pierce didn't adjust well to his new setting. "I never quite fit in and became one of the family," he says. So when Pierce was 12, his father came to get him. Pierce moved onto the ranch with his dad.

"He had another house trailer right next door," Pierce says. "So I lived in my own house trailer from the time I got down there at 12 years old. He would seriously be gone for a month or more at a time, and I would just take care of the ranch myself and get to school and cook my meals and do my laundry and whatever else had to be done. It didn't seem strange to me. It probably seemed strange to other people." Which is to say that by the time Virl Norton saw the ad for the Great American Horse Race in the magazine Western Horseman, 16-year-old Pierce Norton was well prepared to be his dad's crew.

So Virl and Pierce set out from California for the starting line in New York in a 1971 Dodge pickup with loose steering, hauling a camper and a low-end horse trailer that didn't have any horses in it. What it did carry was Lord Fauntleroy, nicknamed Leroy, and a backup mule named Lady Eloise. On May 31, 1976, the Great American Horse Race began. The race was structured like the Tour de France. There was a set course for each day — usually about 35 miles — and the riders were clocked at the start and finish.

At first, Virl's strategy didn't pay off. "There was people going full blast the first day," Pierce says. "Probably rode twice as fast as my dad did. Sooner or later you start to wonder, you know, 'I wonder if this is a good strategy?' I'm thinking, 'If these guys keep it up, there's no way we're going to be able to make up this time.'" But here's another thing you need to know about the Great American Horse Race — and maybe you've been wondering this. Veterinarians accompanied the group, and there were mandatory checks throughout the day. If a horse — or mule — showed any signs of breaking down, even if it just wasn't walking right, the horse — or mule — would have to ride in the trailer until it was healthy again. And that meant penalty time for the riders.

So, as the days went on, more and more horses started breaking down. And more and more riders started getting penalty time. And that wasn't the only thing slowing some teams…"There was plenty of drinking on this thing," Lewis says. "People in the middle of the night screaming and hollering and fighting and 'Where's my girlfriend?' and that sort of thing." And while other competitors were getting into trouble, Lewis says Pierce was "absolutely, positively focused." "I mean, he was busy all the time," Lewis says. "He was doing things. It was a full time job doing all the things he had to do. Laundry, shopping, groceries, cook and all that sort of thing." And with a focused crew and a healthy ride, sure enough..."They had a begrudging respect for the mules sooner or later," Pierce says. Because about a quarter of the way into the race, in Kankakee, Illinois, Virl Norton and Leroy went out ahead of all the Arabians.

"I'm 56 years old now, and, in the 40 years since that race happened, there's not a bigger event in my life." "He'd always said that he hadn't planned on taking the lead that early. Everyone ran their horses down a little bit sooner than he thought, I guess," Pierce says. "You know, soon as we got into the lead, there was a long way to go. But we were going in the right direction. The lead was getting longer." And so, days before the finish, it became clear that a mule was going to win the Great American Horse Race. And on the last day…"There was a whole bank of press photographers and just these cameras flashing and going off like crazy. And some of the other competitors put my dad up on his shoulders and ran him around the fairground a little bit," Pierce says. "I don't know if we ever really had a kind of moment where we did a high-five. He wasn't that kind of guy. He could just look over and nod at me and I would know that he was satisfied with the job that I did."

Virl Norton rides Lady Eloise with Leroy in tow

Winning the race got Virl Norton into newspapers and on TV. It earned him respect among his horse-loving friends for the rest of his life. For Pierce, there was no fame. When the race was over, he went back to high school. He's a scientist now and he says he hasn't ridden a horse — or a mule — in 20 years. But the Great American Horse Race remains special. Virl Norton died in 1995. His son remembers him fondly. "I come to appreciate some stuff kind of later on," he says. "You know my dad raised me kind of on his own, and his best attribute was that he could get more out of a person than they thought they could give. He would give you an opportunity to prove to yourself that you were good."

And in 1976, Virl and Pierce Norton and their mule, Leroy, proved to America that they weren't just good. They were great. *(cited from: https://www.wbur.org/onlyagame/2016/09/09/virl-pierce-norton-horse-mule-race and http://virlnorton.madmoosestudio.com/photos.php?album=2)*

The Funeral of Alexander the Great

As soon as the tracks along which the procession of the funeral of Alexander the Great was to pass were leveled, the magnificent chariot, set out from Babylon. The body of the chariot rested upon two axle-trees, that were inserted into four wheels, made after the Persian manner; the naves and spokes of which were covered with gold, and the felloes plated over with iron. The extremities of the axle-trees were made of gold, representing the muzzles of lions biting a dart. The chariot had four draught beams, or poles, to each of which were harnessed four sets of mules, each set consisting of four of these animals; so that this chariot was drawn by sixty-four mules. The strongest of these creatures, and the largest were chosen on this occasion. They were adorned with crowns of gold, and collars enriched with precious stones and golden bells.

On this chariot was erected a pavilion of entire gold, twelve feet wide, and eighteen in length, supported by columns of the Ionic order, embellished with the leaves of acanthus. The inside was adorned with a blaze of jewels, disposed in the form of shells. The circumference was beautified with a fringe of golden network; the threads that composed the texture were an inch in thickness, and to those were fastened large bells, whose sound was heard at a great distance.

The external decorations were disposed into four relievos. The first represented Alexander seated in a military chariot, with a splendid sceptre in his hand, and surrounded, on one side, with a troop of Macedonians in arms; and on the other, with an equal number of Persians armed in their manner. These were preceded by the king's equerries.

In the second were seen elephants completely harnessed, with a band of Indians seated on the fore-part of their bodies; and on the hinder, another band of Macedonians, armed as in the day of battle.

The third exhibited to the view several squadrons of horse ranged in military array.

The fourth represented ships preparing for a battle.

At the entrance into the pavilion were golden lions, that seemed to guard the passage. The four corners were adorned with statues of gold representing Victories, with trophies of arms in their hands. Under the pavilion was placed a throne of gold of a square form, adorned with the heads of animals, whose necks were encompassed with golden circles a foot and a half in breadth: to these were hung crowns that glittered with the liveliest colours, and such as were carried in procession at the celebration of sacred solemnities.

At the foot of the throne was placed the coffin of Alexander, formed of beaten gold, and half filled with aromatic spices and perfumes, as well to exhale an agreeable odor, as for the preservation of the corpse. A pall of purple wrought with gold covered the coffin. Between this and the throne the arms of that monarch were disposed as he wore them while living.

The outside of the pavilion was likewise covered with purple flowered with gold. The top ended in a very large crown of the same metal, which seemed to be a composition of olive-branches. The rays of the sun, which darted on this diadem, in conjunction with the motion of the chariot, caused it to emit a kind of rays like those of lightning ...

The chariot was followed by the royal guards, all in arms, and magnificently arrayed.

The multitude of spectators of this solemnity is hardly credible; but they were drawn together, as well as by their veneration for the memory of Alexander, as by the magnificence of this funeral pomp, which had never been equaled in the world.

This account is taken from: The Ancient History of Egyptians, Carthaginians, Assyrians, Babylonians, Medes and Persians, Grecians and Macedonians (London c.1830), Vol.3, pp.530-1 *(cited from: https://www.tate.org.uk/art/artworks/bauchant-the-funeral-procession-of-alexander-the-great-t00466)*

Flying Mules

During World War II, British soldiers were sent to the southeast Asian country of Burma (modern-day Myanmar) to fight the Japanese. Burma's terrain was dominated by jungles and mountains, which made it nearly impossible to use modern vehicles to transport supplies. That's were mules came in.

During their earlier excursion into Burma, Wingate's Chindits had used mules to carry ammunition and supplies. All of the pack animals taken in on that first mission had been requisitioned from Indian army artillery units. For the upcoming operations, larger and stronger mules had been imported from Argentina, South Africa and the United States. The newly arrived mules, averaged some 700 pounds in weight. At General Wingate's request, a CG-4A glider was rigged to carry three mules on a test flight. British soldiers built three padded stalls in the test glide. The glider pilot brought along a mechanic armed with an M-1 rifle. Just before take-off he instructed the mechanic: "If any one of those critters starts raising hell up in the sky you shoot him right between the eyes before he kicks our glider apart." The mules proved to be docile passengers throughout the flight.

Eventually more mules were flown in. Four to six mules were loaded into a Dakota aircraft and placed in makeshift bamboo stalls. The mules were typically well-behaved on these flights too.

At one point the entire squadron of transport C-47s was ordered to be grounded. They eventually discovered that the urine from the mules would run through the floor and onto the plane's wires. The order shut down the complete war effort in West China and East Burma until such time that floor boards could be pulled and cables inspected and treated with anti-corrosion chemicals and special grease applied. One can imagine the ruckus it caused at Fourteenth Air Force headquarters when General Chennault was advised that mule urine had shut down the much needed services of his troop carrier unit. The mules had accomplished what the enemy could not!

Sometimes, when troops needed more mules, but there wasn't anywhere for a plane to land, the mules would be parachuted in. This didn't always end so well for the mules, as the jerk of the parachute opening could burst their mesenteric artery. Eventually, a special parachute was created, consisting of an inflatable dinghy, into which the mule would be placed, attached to six parachutes.

But whether the mules were flown, parachuted, or walked in, without them, the troops doubtless would have had a much harder time of it in Burma. As one soldier remarked, "We couldn't have gone half the distances we did and gone half the places we did without the mules." *(cited from: https://www.fold3.com/page/642791606-using-mules-in-burma/ and https://www.ww2gp.org/3mulesInGlider.html and http://www.chindit.net/Mules.html)*

Honky

submitted by: Laura Zellweger, Parishville, New York

Bill is a professional Santa. When Bill went to the north pole (the mall) during the Christmas season his mule, Honky, would stay at his friend Laura's house.

A few years ago Laura started keeping Honky full time. While living with Laura, Honky became invaluable. Laura had a mare who foaled and then, sadly, ended up being euthanized due to EPM and cancer. The colt was only four months old at the time. Honky helped comfort the colt during the weaning process and kind of became his nanny.

The Charge of the Mule Brigade

Although the Battle of Wauhatchie, Tennessee, is not among the better known battles of the Civil War, it nevertheless stands as one of its few significant night assaults. On the evening of October 28, 1863, during the Chattanooga campaign, Confederate troops under the command of General James Longstreet attacked the Federal forces of General John W. Geary. General Joseph Hooker had left Geary's troops to guard the road along which ran the "Cracker Line," the round about route by which Union troops were forced to supply occupied Chattanooga. Although the fighting was disorganized and confused, it raged until 4:00 the following morning and ended in Confederate failure to break the Cracker Line.

Charge of the Mule Brigade

One of the more enduring and amusing stories to emerge from the Battle of Wauhatchie concerns a purported "charge" by a herd of Union mules, who broke loose from their skinners and dashed headlong into Confederate lines. In his account of the engagement, which appears in *Battles and Leaders*, overall Union commander Ulysses S. Grant claimed that Southern troops under General Evander Law mistook the runaway mules for a cavalry charge and fell back in confusion.

As delightful as the anecdote may be, however, there is no real evidence that it ever happened, since Law's men had been driven back by Generals Hector Tyndale and Orland Smith long before the mules slipped their harnesses and began their precipitous flight towards freedom. Nevertheless, the story spread quickly and was accepted as truthful; there was even talk of brevetting the mules as horses. *(cited from: https://www.civilwarpoetry.org/union/battles/mules-exp.html and http://companyqdispatches.blogspot.com/2012/03/amusing-story-charge-of-mule-brigade.html)*

This poem, an obvious parody on Alfred Lord Tennyson's famous "Charge of the Light Brigade," was probably composed shortly after the incident and gained widespread circulation.

Half a mile, half a mile,
  Half a mile onward,
Right through the Georgia troops
  Broke the two hundred.
"Forward the Mule Brigade!
  Charge for the Rebs," they neighed.
Straight for the Georgia troops
  Broke the two hundred.

"Forward the Mule Brigade!"
  Was there a mule dismayed?
Not when their long ears felt
  All their ropes sundered.
Theirs not to make reply,
Theirs not to reason why,
Theirs but to make Rebs fly.
On! to the Georgia troops
  Broke the two hundred.

Mules to the right of them,
Mules to the left of them,
Mules behind them
  Pawed, neighed, and thundered.
Breaking their own confines
Breaking through Longstreet's lines
Into the Georgia troops
  Stormed the two hundred

Wild all their eyes did glare,
Whisked all their tails in air
Scattering the chivalry there,
  While all the world wondered.
Not a mule back bestraddled,
Yet how they all skedaddled --
Fled every Georgian,
Unsabred, unsaddled,
  Scattered and sundered!
How they were routed there
  By the two hundred!

Mules to the right of them,
Mules to the left of them,
Mules behind them
  Pawed, neighed, and thundered;
Followed by hoof and head
Full many a hero fled,
Fain in the last ditch dead,
Back from an ass's jaw
All that was left of them, --
  Left by the two hundred.

When can their glory fade?
Oh, what a wild charge they made!
  All the world wondered.
Honor the charge they made!
Honor the Mule Brigade,
  Long-eared two hundred!

The Real Civil War Mule Brigades

The Lightning Mule Brigade

U.S. Army Colonel Abel Streight in March, 1863 convinced General James Garfield to allow him to organize a cavalry brigade for the purpose of carrying out operations from Tennessee deep into the South. Streight had dealt with northern Alabama Unionists, and felt they could be encouraged and protected, by emulating the operations of Confederate General N. B. Forrest. Thus was born the so-called Union "Lightning Mule Brigade." Streight's plan was risky, but the decision to mount the raiders on mules, and not horses, was a grave mistake. The Union command believed mules would be more sure-footed in the rugged northern Alabama hill country and better able to withstand the rigors of a two hundred mile raid. And, the thinking went, while mules were slower than horses, the raiders had little need for swift mounts, as they were not likely to see any opposition. As soon as the Lightning Mule Brigade disembarked from transports at Eastport, Mississippi, some 400 mules dashed off into the countryside. Some of the escapees were retrieved, others replaced through forage.

Unfortunately for Streight's raiders, the Rebel cavalryman that Streight so admired, General Nathan Bedford Forrest, happened to be in the vicinity. It wasn't long before Forrest was in hot pursuit of Streight's brigade. Forrest's tough veteran cavalrymen relentlessly pursued the Union troops across northern Alabama, guided by the loud braying of the Yankees' mules. The Yankees and Rebels fought a series of small, brutal battles. Although bloodied by Union ambushes, Forrest's men invariably re-grouped and resumed their pursuit, not permitting their quarry to rest. Believing that their wounded comrades were slowing them down, Streight's harried men abandoned them beside the trail with food and blankets. The fitful running fight ground down the slow, balky mules, and they died by the score.

The endurance contest ended near Galesville, Georgia where the raiders destroyed the Round Mountain Iron Works - the mission's only tangible achievement. Forrest's cavalrymen pounced on the exhausted Yankees when they stopped for breakfast after marching all night. Some were sleeping so soundly they could not be rousted to fight, and other dozed off on the skirmish line. Rather than attack, Forrest's men repeatedly circled Streight's raiders to create the impression of overwhelming numbers. The ruse worked. Convinced that he was outnumbered and that his men were in no condition to fight, Streight surrendered. Just 20 foot-sore mules survived. After Streight handed Forrest his sword and his men stacked their arms, Streight learned the depth of Forrest's deception. With just 500 men, Forrest had captured Steight's brigade which was three times larger. Streight demanded that his arms be returned so that he could fight it out, a proposition that amused Forrest, but that he rejected. In his after-battle report, Streight altered the facts: "We were confronted by fully three times our number." (*cited from: https://civilwartalk.com/threads/lightning-mule-brigade.83821/*)

The Hatchet Brigade

John Thomas Wilder (January 31, 1830 – October 20, 1917) was an officer in the Union Army. Wilder received wide attention for his performance in the Tullahoma Campaign. He mounted his brigade on horses and mules that his men appropriated from the local area and moved into the battle with such rapidity that his men soon became known as the "Lightning Brigade", comprising the 17th Indiana Infantry Regiment, the 72nd Indiana Infantry Regiment, the 98th Illinois Infantry Regiment, the 123rd Illinois Infantry Regiment, and the 18th Independent Battery Indiana Light Artillery. They were also known as the "Hatchet Brigade" because Wilder issued them long-handled hatchets to carry instead of cavalry sabers. His men also carried Spencer repeating rifles, which were capable of a rate of fire far greater than their Confederate adversaries. Bypassing Army red tape, Wilder had asked his men to vote on purchasing the rifles and they agreed unanimously. He obtained a loan from his hometown bank and each man of the brigade co-signed a personal loan of $35 ($713 in 2019 dollars) for his rifle. Embarrassed, the Government paid for the weapons before the men expended any of their personal money. On June 24, the Brigade seized and held Hoover's Gap. Despite orders from general Joseph J. Reynolds to fall back to his infantry, which was still six miles away, Wilder decided to hold the position, defeating repeated attempts to dislodge his force until the infantry arrived and winning the most significant battle in the Tullahoma Campaign. The Army of the Cumberland's commanding officer, William Rosecrans soon arrived on the scene. Rather than reprimand Wilder for disobeying orders, he congratulated him for doing so, telling him it would have cost thousands of lives to take the position if he had abandoned it. Wilder was the principal commander of a diversion launched against Chattanooga - artillery bombardments known as the Second Battle of Chattanooga - deceiving the Confederates into thinking the Union army would approach Chattanooga from the north in conjunction with Union forces at Knoxville. *(cited from: https://en.wikipedia.org/wiki/John_T._Wilder)*

Wilder's Lightning Brigade

Bess - The Mine Mule

The following articles, reprinted from 1914 issues of The Seattle Star, relate (with some inaccuracies) the story of the underground deaths of two coal miners, Andrew Churnick and Mike Babchanik. (The miners' names were actually Andrew Chernick and Mike Babcanik. Babcanik was miraculously found alive seven days later.) It is also the story of a mistreated mine mule named Bess. Bess worked 24 hours a day without a rest at a Pacific Coal Company coal mine in Franklin, in east King County. The revelation of the mule's condition came when a reporter went to the mine to cover the accident. The articles were contributed by William Kombol, Manager of Palmer Coking Coal Company located in Black Diamond (King County), Washington.

Reprinted from The Seattle Star, Thursday, February 19, 1914, p. 8
MULES ARE CHEAP; THEREFORE BESS KEEPS ON TOILING
By Fred L. Boalt

FRANKLIN, Feb. 19 -- There is no room in business for sentimental nonsense. If you are to show a balance on the right side of the ledger, you cannot be over-careful of the lives of men or the comfort of mules. Being a practical man, I am led to make these observations after visiting the Cannon mine, here, to find out how Andrew Churnick and Mike Babcanick, experienced miners, died — and why. Viewed sentimentally, the disaster of last Monday was lamentable. One may feel sorry for men and mules that work in mines. But I cannot find that the Pacific Coast Coal Co. was in any way to be blamed for the tragedy. Its business is to GET OUT THE COAL.

When I reached the mouth of the mine I met Toby, the Slav mule-skinner, and Bess, his mule. Never have I seen such a ramshackle animal as this rack of bones. Her wobbly legs are swollen and bleeding. Her emaciated body is a mass of harness sores. Her mangy hide, stretched tight as a drumhead, shows every bone. Between bones are deep cavities where flesh ought to be. She had just strength enough left to drag the cars. "Some Mule," I observed. Toby, the tow-headed, regarded his beast without pride. "Bess he dam' tired," he said. We talked. It seemed Bess was once a fine and prideful mule. Good mules cost money.

Mule experts disagree as to which of two policies brings the best returns on an investment in mules. Some say the better policy is to feed a mule well, and work it reasonable hours, for then it will live long. But the Pacific Coast Coal Co. has found that mules are tough and hard to kill, and that if you work a mule 24 hours a day, it will, while it lasts, do the work of three mules working eight-hour shifts.

Bess, Toby told me, had worked four months, 24 hour shifts! It's hard to believe that even a mule could stand it. And on a diet of hay at that! Toby said Bess snatched ten-minute naps, STANDING UP, between trips! When Bess dies, the company will buy another mule. So much for Bess, who isn't worth bothering about, anyhow.

Pacific Coast Coal Company

Men are different. For one thing, men are not property. They work for wages. If they don't like the job and the attendant risks, they are at liberty to quit. Clearly, it is the right of a coal company to get out as much coal as possible, as cheaply as possible, and to sell it for as much money as possible. Therefore, the company, knowing there was coal at the face of No. 11 chute, was justified in telling Andrew Churnick and Mike Babchanik to go there and dig it. It is true that No. 11 chute was known to be dangerous. For a month the water had been pouring through, and the earth above had been cracking and groaning like a live thing in pain. It is known, too, that the chute's face was perilously near the earth's surface, and that there was gravel, which miners fear as they fear quicksand, ahead. The company didn't know that just above the chute was a bog — a natural catch-basin which drained the hills all about. The company could have known this if it had cared to survey. But surveys cost money. The flow of water increased until one stream was the size of a man's arm. The force of the flow over the inclined floor of the chute was sufficient to flush the coal as fast as it was dug down to the gangway, 400 feet away. This, incidentally, saved the cost of a "bucker," whose duty it is to "buck" the coal down the incline to where it can be picked up by the cars. So Churnick and Babchanik approached the chute in fear. But a job's a job. And $3.80 A DAY WAS ALL THAT STOOD BETWEEN THEIR FAMILIES AND STARVATION.

If you had been on a certain forest trail a mile distant from the mine mouth at 9 o'clock Monday morning, at a point where the road overlooks a natural basin, you could have witnessed what appeared to be a strange and awful phenomenon. The bottom fell out of the basin. Huge trees tottered and crashed down, and were sucked into the abyss. There was a roar of rushing waters, a crushing, crunching, grinding chorus, and then silence.

At that instant two lives were blotted out in the unseen warren below. From the still forest trail you could not guess what was happening in the bowels of the earth beneath your feet. Thousands of tons of water and gravel and boulders and quicksand rushed down into the chute. I think old Earth tried to warn the miners. For this morning the rescue party found the crushed and mangled body of a man, not in No. 11, but in No. 12. He had run for his life.

The flood caught him and his comrade before they had gotten far, and made short work of them. It swept over them. It roared through the cross-cuts. The miners fled before it, snatching at their heels as they fled from cross-cut to cross-cut, from chute to chute, dodging and twisting

Pacific Coast Coal Company Miner

in that underground labyrinth, seeking an avenue of escape. Only the bulkheads at the bottom of the chutes held the flood out of the gangway long enough for the miners to get away. No coal is coming out of the mine today. Only gravel and muck. But, coal or muck, there is no rest for Bess. "Hard luck," said Superintendent of Mines, William Hann."It is not my business to fix the responsibility," said State Mine Inspector, James Bagley. "If," said an old miner, "the company had obeyed the law and made test borings, the water and gravel would have been discovered, and Mike and Andy would be alive today." The state will pay the widows $4,000 each and wash its hands of the whole business. The company may do something handsome in the way of funeral expenses.

Reprinted from The Seattle Star, Friday, February 20, 1914, p. 1

COUNTY HUIMANE SOCIETY TO AID BESS, THE MULE

The King County Humane society promises to put an end to the practice of the Pacific Coast Coal Co., which has found that by working mules in its mines continually without a rest until they die, more work can be accomplished than by working the animals in shifts.

Fred L. Boalt, special writer for The Star, found such a condition upon arriving in Franklin, Wash., to "cover" an accident in the Cannon coal mine. The story appeared in Thursday's Star; and, acting immediately, the humane society assigned Officer Vaupel and Mrs. S. A. Hollabaugh to investigate.

Reprinted from The Seattle Star, Wednesday, February 25, 1914, p. 1

HUMANE AGENT RESCUES BESS; TO MAKE ARREST

"Bess," the mule which worked 24 hours a day in the Pacific Coast Coal Co.'s mine at Franklin, Wash., is enjoying a much-needed rest today as a result of prompt action by the King County Humane society, following publication of an article regarding her in The Star. An arrest will be made at the mine today, as a consequence.

Fred L. Boalt, The Star's special writer discovered "Bess" while "covering" a mine accident at Franklin. He found that the company worked its mules until they die; instead of getting more and working them in shifts. It was cheaper.

Bess the mule at Franklin Coal Mine, King County, March 17, 1914. Photo by Curtis and Miller, Courtesy Washington State Historical Society (28219)

Mrs. S. C. Griggs, secretary of the Humane society, visited the mine with two officers Friday. She immediately ordered Bess to the barn. "The mule had worked two weeks without a rest," Mrs. Griggs said.

Postscript: On St. Patrick's Day, 1914, the Pacific Coast Coal Company hired the famed photographer Asahel Curtis, who had teamed up with William Miller in the firm Curtis and Miller, to take three photos of "Bess" the mule. The photos were shot in the town of Franklin not far from the mine. They were likely taken in order to dispel any remaining public concerns as to the ultimate fate of "Bess." *(cited from: https://www.historylink.org/File/8651)*

Francis the Talking Mule

Francis the mule, was and is, still a favorite comedy. The films were based on a popular book about a military man who meets a mule who can talk. Arthur Lubin, the producer, of the movies later went on to create the Mister Ed TV series. Francis was trained by Will Rogers and apprentice Les Hilton, Mister Ed's trainer. The same technical practice of teaching Francis when to move his mouth was later used on Mister Ed. Mules are very smart and will do what they are asked as long as you are kind and gentle with them. Chill Wills was the original voice of Francis. Paul Fees did the voice in last movie. Francis did 7 movies from 1949 to 1956 starring with character "Peter Sterling" was Donald O'Connor and in the last movie, was Mickey Rooney

This debut of the "Francis" series co-starred Patricia Medina and the United States Army. While on a mission behind enemy lines in Burma, G.I., "Peter", Donald O'Connor, is rescued by a talking mule named Francis. Peter tries to explain that a talking mule rescued him from behind enemy lines, unbelieving superiors take Peter for a crackpot and put him under military arrest. Peter is placed in a padded cell before the pair are recognized for their heroic deeds. Francis comes up with new plans of heroic action. Peter tries to convince his commanding officers that Francis' gift of gab is a credit to the service. Francis stubbornly refuses to talk to outsiders. This makes Peter's job of explaining the crazy situations to the five-star general impossible.

Francis was actually a female mule named Molly. Molly originally hailed from Missouri. Edward D. Frazier of Drexel, Missouri was arguably the best breeder of mules in the country and most likely won more fair championships than any other mule breeder in history. He provided mule mascots for the National Democratic Party and anyone else who needed one of the finest mules available. In 1949, a Missouri news photographer, named Jack Hackethorn, apparently heard that Universal Studios was looking for a mule. He bought Molly from Frazier Farms for a reported $200 and convinced Universal to spring for the $450 air fare to fly her out to Hollywood for a screen test. Competing against eight other mules from across the U.S.,

Molly was selected, it is said, for her "appeal, great personality, long eyelashes and photogenic face." Molly had to go on a strict diet after her first movie; she gained 200 pounds because the cast and crew kept feeding her carrots and whatever else she wanted, spoiling her. Everyone loved the mule!

For a simple mule, Francis certainly got around—to the jungles of Burma in "Francis" (1950), the Santa Anita race track in "Francis Goes to the Races" (1951), West Point in "Francis Goes to West Point" (1952), and to New York City in "Francis Covers the Big Town" (1953). He also joined the WACs in "Francis Joins the WACS" (1954), the US Navy in "Francis in the Navy" (1955) and solved a murder mystery in "Francis in the Haunted House" (1956). In 1952 Francis even made an appearance on the popular game show "What's My Line?" The Francis series helped to keep the financially struggling Universal-International studio afloat.

Kids loved Francis in the early 1950s. Dell published a series of "Francis the Talking Mule" comic books, and there was also a syndicated "Francis" strip in the newspaper comic written by Frank Thomas and drawn by Cliff Rogerson.

Donald O'Connor is not known to have ever spoken ill of the mule (even though Francis was receiving more fan mail than him). Not wanting to expose the fact that Francis was actually a female, he referred publicly to Francis in the male reference. "Francis never attempted to hurt me in any way or step on me, even when I would walk behind him and hold on to his tail. He was the most docile animal I've ever worked with. Francis had three understudies, but nine out of ten times, they'd balk and he'd have to do it anyway. He was a trouper."

Molly - "Francis" - was the very first recipient of the American Humane Association Annual Patsy Award in 1950 *(cited from: http://horsefame.tripod.com/francis.html and https://www.findagrave.com/memorial/95415289/the_talking-mule-francis)*

Festus and Ruth

If you paid close attention to the television show Gunsmoke, you know that Festus took care of mules and all their names were Ruth - even if they were jacks. Festus' mule was always a jack but HIS name was always RUTH! In the words of Festus Hagen, here's why.....

You ask how come I call my old mule, Ruth, when in fact the solemn truth is that he's a jack, and not no jenny, that's for sure. Well, they's no call for you to know, but since you asked, I'll tell you so just settle back and heed to what I say.

It started in 1861, the war, well it had just begun to be a war. I wasn't much, so to speak, a mule skinner, not one to seek fame nor fortune, especially in no war.

Now, every man's got a pride. Most times it's deep inside about his job and mine was attending mules. My favorite was a long-eared jenny. Now, I reckon you'll think that I'm a ninny 'cause I loved her just like I'd love my mother. She was faithful, stout and she was smart, and friend, she had lots of heart. If she'd been a man, I'd a loved her like a brother.

Well, we'd fought back with all we had, but still the war was a going bad, for in '64 Schofield hit us Tennessee boys hard, and just thirty miles away, at dawn, near Spring Hill on a early 'morn, five generals that wore Confederate gray had chitin's and bacon and eggs and grits. Lord, they'd planned to give 'em fits but the tide of war just went the other way. The five brave men that led Hood's charge was met by a artillery barrage that mowed 'em down just like so much hay.

Now, somebody had to get them men and, by golly I can't remember when I've ever been so proud as I was that day. "Just take 'ol Ruth," the Captain said, and when it got dark, I slowly led my jenny to the Harpeth Rivers bank. I'd found them boys in gray and when on Ruth's back they stiffly lay, I started back, but then my spirit sorta sank. A dad-blamed sentry opened fire and them Yankee's did conspire to add me to their list of casualties. Well, 'ol Ruth, she just plowed along not a listening to the bullet song, just brushed 'em off like they was a swarm of bee's.

Well, somehow we got back that night, and I thanked God I was alright. I'd brought them boys from where they was a laying. I hadn't even got a scratch, so I lit my pipe and when the match flared up, I seen 'ol Ruth was just a swaying'. Blood was running down her side. My throat choked up and then I cried, and she looked at me and her eyes was soft and brown. She seemed to say, "Now, don't cry for me, we had a job to do, you see!" And, then 'old Ruth just seemed to slide right down.

There's a marker that I put on her grave that reads, "Here lies a mule that gave her life and that's the truth. Now, every mule I'll ever own will bare your name. So, be it known while I'm alive, they'll always be a Ruth " Yeah, they'll always be a Ruth. *(cited from: http://www.randyspecktacular.com/2011/06/ode-to-mule.html)*

Three Mules

There is a man wandering around California with three mules. He has a name, but he prefers to go by Mule. Police departments throughout the state know his name. They inevitably get calls from residents who wonder why a man with three mules is sleeping on the side of the road, and from time to time they have to go and investigate and decide whether or not to ticket him. He has had so many run-ins with the police that he has a lawyer. (The lawyer knows Mule's name.) The filmmaker John McDonald, who has spent hundreds of hours filming Mule on his journeys, and who helped Mule set up a Facebook page, knows Mule's name as well.

Mule is 67 years old and has slept outside with his three mules for the last 10 years, though he's lived his nomadic lifestyle for much longer than that - 29 years on and off. He got his first mule in Spokane, Washington, so that he could carry more supplies with him into the bush than his meager, rail-thin frame can handle. With his first mule, and then a second, and a third, he could load up on supplies to last him for much longer in the undeveloped parts of the American West, so he'd only have to resurface in towns to resupply once every month or so before once again disappearing. Soon he realized the world he inhabited was changing. While he sought solitude, he kept bumping into development. Land he had passed through was no longer public and was vanishing behind fences. Everywhere he looked, he saw ever more roads and cars. He knew then that he wanted to speak up about what he was seeing.

Filmmaker John McDonald was at first interested in Mule as a documentary subject, after a few months of filming, he confessed to Mule, "I really believe a lot in what you're doing. In spite of the documentary, I would probably want to support you and what you're doing, and I respect you." When McDonald first met Mule over a year ago, Mule was carrying with him three cell phones, two voice recorders, a digital camera, and a tablet. He already had his website, 3mules.com, up and running, but didn't know how to update it. When Mule agreed to let McDonald film him, he asked for a favor in return: McDonald had to teach Mule how to use the tools that he carried with him. There is something deeply beautiful about how Mule is living. Just read through his Facebook page to see how much people admire his deliberate wanderings and his simple, poetic insights. *(cited from: https://www.theatlantic.com/technology/archive/2013/09/there-is-a-man-wandering-around-california-with-3-mules/279495/)*

Note: Mule is now 72 years old and followed by approximately 50,000 people on Facebook! His Facebook page is: 3 Mules. The movie is in process: www.3mulesmovie.com

Ole Pete

Story below submitted by: Doye Rowland, Eagleville, Tennessee

Old Pete was our mule. Our father, Grady Granville Rowland, we think acquired old Pete in 1958 from our Uncle Willie B Rowland, whom we call Uncle B. Uncle B farmed in Bedford County, Tennessee near the community of Rover. We admired our Uncle B as a good horse trader who loved horses and mules, but, more importantly, he was recognized and admired for his love of God.

Daddy needed some horsepower to help work land and maintain the property, so he purchased Ole Pete. Ole Pete was used to plow and cultivate, but he did not pull the plow very much. It was too hard on him. I do remember Bill and I breaking the garden with Pete with a one bottom turning plow. We worked together to make one working man. Bill guided the plow by the handles and I had the reins and guided the mule. We mostly used Pete to cultivate rows in the garden or in the various tobacco patches. Daddy called the cultivator a harrow, but I think it may be more accurately termed a one horse cultivator. The cultivator had three cultivating points. It would be pulled through the rows of the garden or the various tobacco patches. Pete would pull the cultivator down one side of the row and then back down the other side of the same row. Bill would direct the cultivator with the wooden handles and I would guide the mule. As we went up the rows we would throw the dirt toward the plants. The dirt would smother small weeds close the plants and the extra dirt would help hold moisture during the summer weather. The cultivator had a metal guard held up from the ground by a wire. If desired, we could unfasten the metal guard letting it drag along between the cultivator and plants. The guard could protect small plants from the soil being tilled by the cultivator. The use of the cultivator saved us hours or days of hoeing the weeds.

Bill, Daddy (Grady G. Rowland), and Doye

Grady G. Rowland and Betty Sue Rowland

As my brother Bill and I grew older, it became our job to work with Ole Pete. By then, Daddy began to use the advantage of our age, strength, and energy. He rented government regulated tobacco allotments from some neighbors down the road. We did not rent with cash but by shares. I did not realize that we were share croppers until years later when our class read about share croppers in history books. The land owners would receive 2/3 of the profit and we would receive 1/3 of the profit. We had a small .25 acre allotment of tobacco crop. We worked Mrs. Walls allotment of about .5 acres. We worked Mr. Ghee's allotment of about .6 acre. Later we worked a 2 acre allotment on a farm that my mother's parents bought. This farm was farther away. My grandfather had a tractor to help work that acreage. Rather than to haul Ole Pete to the closer farms we would walk him down the public road to the farms. When we got close to the destination, we would cut and go across private properties to cut some distance. As we walked him, leading by the

Fred, Brent, Doye, Bill, Betty Sue, and Grady Rowland

bridle, Pete would stop to eat grass or leaves from the bushes. I don't think Pete respected us as much as a grown person. As we got older Bill lead Pete and it was just the two of them. Once we arrived at the tobacco patch, we began the row by row cultivation. This was perceived by us to be a great blessing because, it reduced hoeing time and made the soil looser for any hoeing that was needed. I think hoeing is a major contributor to why my back hurts while I write this information. When the cultivator gets to the end of the row, it is time to turn Pete around and get him positioned for the next row. This is an awkward process with Pete. I was not as forceful with him as a grown man would have been. He took every advantage that I allowed him. You had to keep things timely and immediately turn him around very promptly and business like or he would get distracted. If Pete steps on a tobacco plant during the turn-around, that would be a plant which would not be sold in the fall. Daddy would be sure to notice.

As Bill and I got older and left home, Fred and Brent took our places. I was not there during much of their experiences. Fred would have had more responsibility as the older of the two. Both say they often rode Pete from the tobacco patch to home. Bill and I were not allowed, nor were we interested in that ride. Brent tells that he was riding Pete from the tobacco patch, and Pete abruptly stopped. Pete saw a snake in their walkway that Brent didn't see. Once Brent saw the snake they went wide around him. I think both Daddy and Ole Pete mellowed out as they aged.

Keep reading for more Ole Pete stories from the rest of the family.

Story below submitted by: J. Brent Rowland, Rockvale, Tennessee

My earliest recollection of Ole Pete was from the time that I was about 8 or 9 years old in the early 1960's. Ole Pete was our family mule. I grew up in the country on a small farm and we had milk cows, hogs, chickens, goats, always a cat and a couple dogs, and of course we had Pete. Pete was a constant. The dogs, cat, and milk cows weren't exactly "family" but they all had names and that gave them a certain status above the hogs, chickens and goats, but with Pete, that was one name and face that never changed throughout my childhood up to the time I left home.

The barn where Ole Pete lived.

Pete had a pretty easy life most of the time. Daddy only used him to plow the garden and the small tobacco patch. Pete didn't like pulling the plow and when it was time for him to pull it, he would hide out at the back end of the pasture. He was a sucker for a small bucket of corn and would always get caught that way. When I was really small I would get to ride Pete while he pulled the plow, but as I got older I had to help my older brothers as they "manned" the plow and I would hold the reins to help steer him and turn him around at the end of the rows. Daddy would do the really hard work of "breaking the ground" in the spring but my older brothers mostly inherited the job harrowing the weeds between the rows as the crop began to grow. Manning the reins was stressful as Pete knew we were just boys and would try to take advantage of us by stealing a bite of something in the next row over as we turned around at the end of the rows.

Pete had his own stall in the barn and his own pasture with special gates. They had to be special because Pete was a "skilled locksmith" in that he would use his tongue and lips to unchain a gate and was even able to untwist a wire when it was used to lock a gate. He did this on multiple occasions and my parents would marvel at his skill. He was on one occasion, able to unlock the feed room and help himself to the crushed corn. My parents were afraid he would gorge himself if left to his desires, but their greatest concern was that one day Pete would get out and just "leave the country". They were always hearing about some horse or mule that got out and was found 20 miles away if ever found at all. Pete was important to the family's livelihood so it was a big deal when he was discovered to be loose. It was "all hands on deck" and always a huge ordeal to finally corral him back through the gate.

Little did we know that this concern that Pete might fly the coop was completely unwarranted. Daddy finally decided it was time to sell Ole Pete since he was getting pretty old by mule standards. He decided to quit growing tobacco, to pay someone to break the garden with their tractor in the spring, and he bought a tiller to plow the weeds out of the garden. Pete had outlived his usefulness. He was able to sell Ole Pete to a family located a few miles away on a different road. Daddy loaded Pete up in the truck and delivered him as part of the deal. The next morning Pete was standing at the gate trying to "pick the lock" to get back into his pasture, so Daddy loaded him up and redelivered him and told the new owners that they really need to wire the gate tight. They said that they would this time for sure......next morning there stood Pete. This happened twice more, before Ole Pete just up and died. Maybe he died of home sickness, a broken heart, or maybe because he was just an old worn out mule....we'll never really know. One thing we do know is that we never really had to worry about Ole Pete just running off, because he would have just gotten homesick and come back home.

Story below submitted by: Micheal Rowland (son of Fred Rowland), Eagleville, Tennessee

Ole Pete as I understand it, brought the yellow looking flowers to the Morgan Road area... it seems like someone told me that once. Granddaddy (Grady G. Rowland) got Pete somewhere else. Can't remember how far away it was from Morgan Rd. As I know the story, Granddaddy noticed lots of little pretty yellow flowers there - he'd never see those on the Rowland farm before. He walked Pete to his new home on Morgan Rd and when he got there, he began to work Pete in the field - pretty hard too. Next year, those same kind of flowers were growing in the field Pete hung out in. Granddaddy said, "Pete brought them there from"... I can't remember where Pete came from.

Story below submitted by: J. Brent Rowland, Rockvale, Tennessee

Michael, I never heard that story about the yellow flowers, but I suspect it would be what we called chigger weeds. Perhaps Pete ate them and deposited the seeds here and there....perhaps? .....or maybe not.

Story below submitted by: Micheal Rowland (son of Fred Rowland), Eagleville, Tennessee

I just saw my Dad (Fred Rowland) and he said Pete came from Rover, Tennessee. He said granddaddy brought him back in the back of a pickup truck. He sad that Brent Rowland and him use to ride Pete when they were little, and I learned this... "Ghee" meant to go left, and Pete would go left. "Yeah" meant to go right, and so that's what Pete would do, and "Whoa" meant to stop. Apparently we had a relative in Rover, some uncle. That's all I know.

Story below submitted by: Doye Rowland, Eagleville, Tennessee

Daddy (Grady G. Rowland) used to say that we did not have the "4 o'clock" flowers on the road side and in the pasture until old Pete came to live in our barn lot. These are a light pink flower close to the ground that easily and quickly spreads. I think by dropping seeds each year. If this timing is true, I suspect it had to originate from old Pete's manure. Daddy used to complain about his boyhood chore of day after day making billets from wood his older brothers would saw and bring to the barn lot for his billet making. After all the years, you could still hear his frustration as he talked about it. Billets are lengths of unfinished wood that have been split to appropriate sizes to make wooden handles for various tools. I would imagine that many of his billets for tool handles would come from such hardwoods as ash and red oak. These hardwoods would split well and were often used in wooden handles. Daddy would use a fro and a wooden club to split the wood into little squares of various lengths which would later be turned by lathe, in town, into tool handles. His daddy would haul the load to Murfreesboro, Tennessee to sell. There and back was a long day's trip.

A load of wooden billets. Mule from Doye Rowland's wife Betty Rowland's family tree. (See Puckett story page 120)

Story below submitted by: Pam Kephart Ludwig, Nashville, Tennessee

I don't doubt that Ole Pete likely came from my Granddaddy Willie B's mule stock. He preferred a mule to a horse when it came to working the farm. He was very good to his animals and they would in turn be very good to him. He was always able to just talk to his animals and they would do what he wanted. But, I don't know the Ole Pete story or mule. I checked with my Mom and she didn't know Ole Pete either. However, I will share a funny mule story. When my grandparents moved from Morgan Road to Rover, Tennessee, it was very hard on the entire family. The Rowlands had never been separated. Anyway, Granddaddy Rowland (Granville Eugene Rowland) came to see my grandfather (Willie B - the B stands for nothing). At that time, Willie B had a blind mule. Apparently Granville Eugene & Willie B were standing in the barn lot talking when the blind mule walked up behind them and laid his head on Granville Eugene's shoulder which scared Granville to death. He yelled and ran away. Apparently the mule was rather large and it really scared him.

Puckett General Store 1904-1952

submitted by: Betty Rowland (Puckett), Eagleville, Tennessee

In 1904, J.N. Puckett and his son, Will, built a "modern" two-story general store on Hwy 99 about half the distance between the Rockvale and Eagleville, Tennessee communities. General stores provided great convenience to rural communities. Puckett's General Store offered groceries, dry goods, dress goods, shoes, furniture, rugs, carpets, hardware, farm tools, jewelry, drugs, and an extensive millinery department operated on the store's mezzanine by Mrs. Will (Allie) Puckett. The store also bought and sold chickens, butter, hides, furs, and eggs from local residents. The store expanded to include two peddler wagons which were actually general supply stores on wheels. There was also a regular freight wagon pulled by two mules, which was on the road daily to Murfreesboro, Tennessee or Nashville, Tennessee to carry the goods which were gathered at the store.

The papers reported that the freight wagon pulled by the two mules held the record for the largest load of eggs transported at 90 cases of eggs in one load. The cases were approximately 25 inches long and each held 30 dozen eggs. A special tool called an egg crate maker was used to assemble the wooden cases. The machine held the end pieces and center divider in place while the bottom was nailed on with 3 penny nails. The foot pedal was used to flip the box making it easy to attach the sides.

Betty Rowland's Grandfather Arville Woodard and Uncle Bradley Woodard and mules of Smith County, TN. 1940.

Now, Mr. Editor, permit me to raise the curtain just a little and give you a peep at the amount of actual labor and business that is carried on there at this country story. They have two market wagons in connection with this store running every day, which are simply general supply stores on wheels; also a regular freight wagon which is kept constantly on the road from this place to Nashville or Murfreesboro carrying the marketing which is gathered up every day at this place. These wagons are run by clean, honorable gentlemen who buy and pay the highest prices for all kinds of marketing and country produce. In 1906 they claim to have handled 49,317 dozen eggs, or 1644 cases about five and one-half car loads, receiving $7,160.21 in cash for same. They handled chickens and butter in like proportions, also hides and furs of all kinds simply in abundance. They carried on their freight wagon 90 cases of eggs or 30 dozen each, said to have been the largest load of eggs ever handled into Murfreesboro in one load. This building, too large for a country business, as you might possibly think, is now much too small to accommodate their business.

Article from Home Journal Newspaper. 1907

Two milliners (hat makers) with the Puckett & Son General Store peddler's wagon and mules.

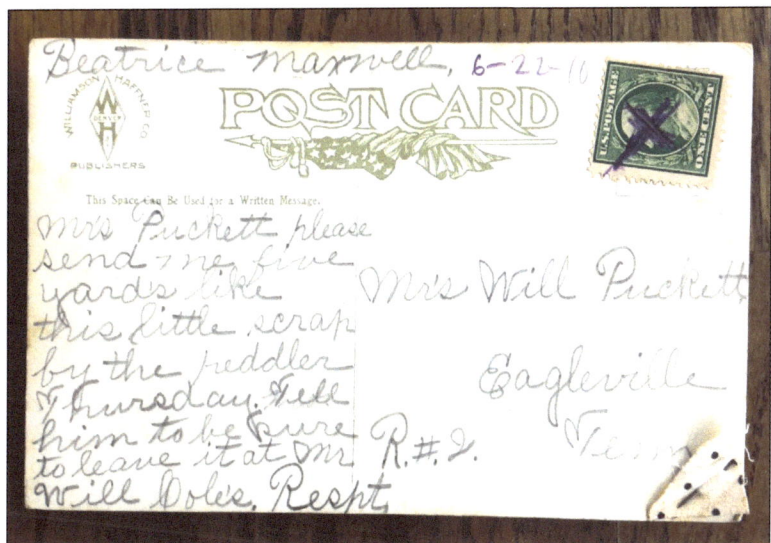

Postcard sent to Puckett General Store ordering more fabric. "Mrs. Puckett, please send me five yards like this little scrap by the peddler Thursday. Tell him to be sure to leave it a Mr. Will Bole's. Respects, Beatrice Maxwell" June 22, 1910

Roanie - Spirit Led

submitted by: *Doug Bennett*

A friend who owned a Christian Retreat facility once asked if my two son's and I would pack a group of his board members into a camping spot on the back of their property for a overnight campout. We borrowed two more mules from my friend Jo Bob and with the camp's two horses and our mules we had just enough to pack the camp in the night before and then return to the retreat facility to carry riders to the camp site the next morning. As is usual we got a late start and ended up getting to the camp site just before dark. When we had unloaded packs and set up the tents, it was dark....very dark. No moon and overcast. You couldn't see your hand at arms length. But my oldest son, Young and I still needed to lead the string out so we could meet up with the riders in the morning at the trailhead. Saying good bye to my son, James and a camp employee, we began to pick our way back towards the facility. I lead the way on my faithful mount, Roanie on a trail that was frankly really not a horse trail at all, but rather just a barely visible game trail, even in good light. Certain shadows and outlines made me believe that, though I couldn't see a thing, my mule was headed back exactly the way we had come. It was necessary to hold my free hand out in front of my face , so as to not be knocked off by low lying, impossible to see, tree branches. Along the trail we went for some 45 minutes or so when suddenly Roanie made a sharp right turn. Up until now I was amazed at how well we were doing and what incredible eye sight mules must have to see that well in the dark. But suddenly it appeared that Roanie had got it all wrong and was heading in the wrong direction. Wanting to correct the error and being pretty sure I knew where we were, I lightly took hold of the reins for the first time and obediently Roanie turned left. Suddenly we were completely surrounded by thick oak brush....in all directions, with nothing even remotely resembling a trail. For what seemed hours we stumbled around in the darkness, crashing through branches, being whipped and scratched in the faced, having my hat knocked off and finally having to dismount in order to pick our way through, hoping to stumble back on the trail. Finally we could go no further.

Exhausted and realizing that I couldn't afford to let my male ego drive us any further, I had to admit we were lost. Our only option was to spend the night out in the open. If we survived the night, we could ride out and meet our riders in the morning rather than that night as we had planned.

When I say survive, I was under no illusion of how serious our situation could turn if it got very cold. Every year, many more people die of hypothermia than just about all other outdoor activities combined. Having taught Hunters Education and survival for a number of years I took our circumstances very serious. I had once been on a trail ride where another father and son had gone out on their own, gotten lost and were forced to spend the night out without a fire on a very chilly September night. The father was shaking violently the next morning when they spotted a ranch house and were able to get to it before it was too late. Here we were without my survival pack, which I never go without. We had no flash light and nothing to keep us warm. I did have a lighter I carried on my saddle for emergencies and we used the illuminated dials on our "Timex" watches to see our way around. The problem was we were in the middle of very dry oak brush that had already dropped their leaves. The wind was just strong enough that a "white man's fire" was out of the question. Only a small fire to warm ourselves was possible and in time the wind picked up enough that we had to extinguish that. That sleepless night, I wrapped my arms around my son's 6 foot plus frame and prayed that his trembling would stop and the pain in his legs would subside. The long night finally began to end with dawn's first hues of light in the east. Young had warmed enough to finally drift asleep, and God graciously kept me awake to keep us both warm. With the light we quickly saddled our mounts and rode back down the hill where we picked up the trail and were back at the facility within an hour. It turned out to be "no big deal", as so often is the case, but was a miserable night spent out none the less.

As we were riding in, the Holy Ghost began to minister to me a very obvious but valuable insight. He said to me that He was like that mule. He was able to see what was ahead even when we couldn't. That as long as I let Him have the reins He would lead us safely where we needed to go. The moment I took hold of the reins to go the way I thought we should go, we got lost. Now as believers our detour can only last a "night", and when the "light" comes again we can quickly come back to the right path. When we realize that we have gone astray, it is vital we acknowledge it, repent and then wait on God to correct our error. Like I said obvious, and maybe over simplified, but how often do we get off track when God is leading us exactly where we should be going. Why do we really think we know best? Sometimes life to me is like a "spiritual minefield". If we don't listen to the guidance of the Holy Spirit's leading we can blow our foot off or worse! Simple lesson? Maybe, but one I find I still struggle with. The Bible says "sheep know the voice of the shepherd, and a strangers voice they will not follow". Sometimes life and our decisions are serious enough that we can't afford not to get His leading. Remember, the Devil, the world and even our flesh has it's own agenda. The Shepherd knows the way we should go, sometimes we're better off when we sit down and wait for the light than to charge on when we know we are off.

Ole Tobe

submitted by: Patricia A. Rowland (Porter), Arlington, Tennessee

Julius and Sara Louise Porter (Webb)

Green Buckboard wagon similar to the one Ole Tobe pulled.

The field Ole Tobe grazed in and often escaped from with Sunny, the walking horse.

Ole Tobe was a mule we had when I was a little girl. I remember Tobe was a smart mule. He could get through any gate and any lock Dad, Julius Porter, would put on a gate. We had 11 horses, including him, with ponies included in that 11. He was continually getting them all out. He would get the gate unlocked and they would all follow him right through. We had neighbors who would alert us to their where abouts.

My Dad had a buckboard wagon that we would decorate every May for the parade in Franklin, Tennessee. He would hook Tobe up to it and we would all ride in the parade with Ole Tobe. Tobe's companion among our horses was a walking horse named Sunny. They were like two partners in crime. They were always together side by side out in the pasture, never far from one another. My older brother would ride Sunny in the parade in front of Tobe, pulling us in the buckboard wagon. Dad would purposely hold Tobe back and let Sunny and my brother get up ahead of us. Tobe would stop and raise his ears up and start his whinny. The crowd loved it and so Dad would hold him back several times in the parade just to get him to show off, as he called it.

Sterlin the Appy Mule

submitted by: Beth Davis, Millington, Tennessee

Once Sterlin, my Appy mule and I went to the Chuckwagon races in Clinton, Arkansas. I had entered us in the Snowy River Race. I had heard a little about how it was challenging. It wasn't until I got there that I began to wonder what did I get myself into. The next morning was the first race, Sterlin was calm. When the starting pistol shot, he didn't even spook. We took off and were half way down the field, when I looked back and the other riders were still trying to get on their horses. I was like, I got this! Then they all came flying by us and we were eating their dust. I didn't know it was a timed event. When Sterlin and I got to the main field everyone was gone and we were the only ones running. We finally arrived at the finish line and were told to hurry and get off the field so they could set up for the next race.

The next day I asked if we could still run but was told we had disqualified ourselves. I joked with the guy that my plan was to start at the bottom of the hill, to get a head start. He said, "No, you need to start at the creek.", which was almost at the finish line. We laughed about it and he went ahead and put us through to the next race. It was fun but we won't be doing that again. Next year we did the Mule Race, where we actually had a chance. That's what I like about my mule. I raised him from my Appy mare. We have the best bond. He loves me and I him. I love going home and hearing him bray when he hears my voice. I say, "Hello Sterlin." And he perks up them big ears like, "I see you Mama." He takes care of me on the trails or anywhere we go.

Lightning

submitted by: Jennifer Wasson, Copemish, Michigan

In 2017, then six year old Lillian, of Copemish, Michigan, convinced her parents to buy a mini mule at an Amish auction....because he was cute. Since then, Lightning has provided lots of experiences and maybe a few bruises. Lillian and Lightning got along fairly well right away, grown adults were another story. He disliked adults and would try to avoid them till feeding time, but even then, only Lillian could pet him.

It wasn't long before Lillian was showing her mule. In the summer of 2018 Lightning was entered in the local fair for their Mule class. Lillian left home with her Mom to drop off the goats she was going to show too; leaving Dad home to bring Lightning. Three hours later Lillian and her Mom received a phone call from a very crabby Dad who had been trying to catch Lightning all that time. Dad had tried every trick and bribe in the book! At this point, the only way Lightning was going to make it to the show was if Lillian went home to catch him. So Lillian and her Mom made the 40 minute drive home. Upon arrival Lillian hopped out of the truck and walked directly out to the pasture where Lightning walked right up to her. She hooked the lead rope and walked him out to the trailer. In the mean time her Mom had to try and calm down a very sweaty and crabby Dad that had lost a fight with a mule. After that adventure, Lightning wore a halter when turned out.

One day the next summer Lillian's Mom heard some groaning coming from the pasture. Lightning had gotten his halter caught on an old spreader in the field and he had flipped over trying to free himself. In the process he twisted his halter tightly - cutting off his air supply. After several attempts of trying to free him, Lillian's brother came to the rescue and was able to pick Lightning up and flip him back over. Lightning was given all sorts of extra attention....and his halter was removed! Ever since that day the mule loves other family members. It's like he knows he was saved. He now lets the entire family pet him and love on him.

The Joys of Mule Ownership

Maria Wachter, Horse Nation's resident mule whisperer, meets a lot of folks out on the trail who ask her: why mules? Here are her top five responses.

1, Mules will always keep you humble.

If you have a big ego and you end up buying a mule, your ego will be knocked down a few notches. Does your mule load into every trailer, no matter what, and do you like to boast about it? Do it in front of someone you just met and watch in disbelief as your mule suddenly forgets how to load. They will take every opportunity to make a fool out of you, so you better have a good sense of humor since you will be the brunt of jokes.

2. Mules will always keep you safe… if you can stay on their back, that is.

A lot of people have the misconception of a mule being their 1200-pound babysitter that will keep them from all harm. The thing is, mules are very smart and have a great self-preservation instinct. They DO NOT at any circumstance want to get themselves hurt or to put themselves in a situation where they could die. They will keep themselves safe, whether you're on their back or not. That includes jumping 30 feet sideways at a potential mule-eating bush, or bolting away at a dead run from an angry water bottle/bicyclist/plastic bag/dog/whatever else could kill them. If you have a really good seat, you may not get hurt, but if you're a rider getting back into the sport because you've been hurt/lost your confidence/lost your stirrups and confidence at the same time, you might be unpleasantly surprised. A horse will jump off a cliff for you, but a mule will watch as you go plummeting off the edge while he's sitting high and dry.

Maria Wachter on her two mules, Bartholomule and Smokey Joe. Photo by Hal Long

3. If you end up getting a mule so you have a pack animal that you can use for hunting, you might be disappointed when that said mule is petrified of the smell of blood.

Some mules will pack anything, some mules will lose their minds when they smell blood. Yes, most of them can be trained eventually to get over this but for the guy/girl that only rides twice a year: one to leg their mule up for hunting season and two for the actual hunt, you might be very frustrated and let down and you might even lose your cool so much that you will have the urge to hunt your mule instead of that deer.

4. Mules are not stubborn.

They are extremely smart and will, a lot of times, outsmart their owner. If you own a mule you will constantly have to be one step ahead of them and constantly be in a state of trying to outsmart them. It's like conquering a video game, mastering an instrument or something of the sort to me. Once you figure one out, each one will be easier and easier. They keep me thinking and always impress me when they outsmart me.

5. Once you figure out your mule and your mule figures out you, you will realize why so many people have mules.

They become extremely loyal and trustworthy and their personalities are so enjoyable. Their sure-footedness and brains under saddle will ease you even in the trickiest of trails. They will keep you laughing and bring a smile to your face even if you're having a terrible day. Plus, who can resist their ears?!

Go riding — on a mule! *(cited from: https://www.horsenation.com/2019/02/20/5-truths-about-riding-mules/)*

What is Your Mule Personality?

Are you a Mule Aficionado? Are you so cool that you can ride a mule like The Duke? Do Mules bring a smile to your face and make you He Haw? Or maybe you're The Mule Whisperer. Take this quiz and find out! Choose the statements you think best describe a mule and give yourself the points for that statement.

1. Mules can be used in exactly the same sports as horses - under saddle, in harness, for cutting, roping or dressage.

☐ True ☐ False

2. Mules are highly patient, sober and tolerant.

☐ True ☐ False

3. A mule is courageous, vigorous and strong.

☐ True ☐ False

4. Mules are resistant to diseases and insects.

☐ True ☐ False

5. A mule is less intelligent in comparison to its parents.

☐ True ☐ False

6. Horses eat less than mules do.

☐ True ☐ False

7. Mules rarely have hoof problems.

☐ True ☐ False

8. Mules no not have a strong sense of self preservation.

☐ True ☐ False

9. Mules move differently than horses.

☐ True ☐ False

10. Mules are loaded with personality.

☐ True ☐ False

11. Mules do not live longer than horses.

☐ True ☐ False

12. Horses can be handled in large groups more easily than mules.

☐ True ☐ False

Tally Your Answers

1. _____ True - 2 points/False - 0 points

2. _____ True - 3 points/False - 0 points

3. _____ True - 1 point/False - 0 points

4. _____ True - 4 points/False - 0 points

5. _____ True - 0 points/False - 2 points

6. _____ True - 0 points/False - 4 points

7. _____ True - 1 point/False - 0 points

8. _____ True - 0 points/False - 3 points

9. _____ True - 4 points/False - 0 points

10. _____ True - 3 points/False - 0 points

11. _____ True - 0 points /False - 1 point

12. _____ True - 0 points/False - 2 points

_____ **TOTAL**

Results

30 - 23 points: You are a Mule Aficionado! You know a lot of interesting mule trivia. If you don't have a mule you NEED a mule!

14 - 7 points: You're a Real He Haw! You enjoy the personality of a mule….but you are not sure that they are better than a horse.

22 - 15 points: You're a Mule Whisperer! Mules like you and you like mules

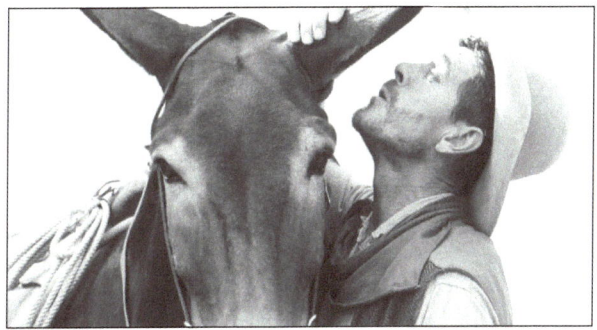

6 - 0 points: You're The Duke! You are the epitome of cool – so you would ride a mule but maybe you are not ready to own one.

My Mule Story

Write your name above and tell your story.

Sources

WHAT IS A MULE

https://spana.org/blog/what-is-a-mule-13-things-you-didnt-know/
http://www.lovelongears.com/about_mules.html
https://animals.mom.me/tell-difference-between-mule-hinny-9758.html
Amy K. McLean, NC State University Equine Extension/ Animal Science Raleigh, NC

MAKING A MULE

https://www.energie-cheval.fr/en/menu-secondaire/la-filiere/anes-mulets/races-mulassieres-du-poitou/
https://spiritedhorse.wordpress.com/2017/12/23/the-standard-of-ur/
http://www.macroevolution.net/horse-hybrids.html
https://www.leroyvandyke.com/p/mules
https://pethelpful.com/horses/Mules-And-Other-Hybrids-About-Equine-Crosses
http://imh.org/exhibits/online/breeds-of-the-world/africa/donkey/
https://www.ruralheritage.com/mule_paddock/donkeys.htm
https://www.ruralheritage.com/new_rh_website/resources/mules_donkeys/mules_donkeys_main.shtml
http://imh.org/exhibits/online/breeds-of-the-world/europe/mule/
https://thefarmatwalnutcreek.com/horses-draft-mule.html
A History of the Percheron Horse, Alvin Howard Sanders, 1917
The Missouri Mule, Melvin Bradley, 1993
Pony Tracks, Frederic Remington, 1895

MULE TRAITS - BEHAVIOR

https://www.muleranch.com/mule-saddle-everything-you-need-to-know/
http://imh.org/exhibits/online/breeds-of-the-world/europe/mule/
https://paintedqhfarm.weebly.com/mule-facts.html
https://www.ruralheritage.com/new_rh_website/resources/mules_donkeys/mules_donkeys_main.shtml
https://americanmuleassociation.org/differences-with-horses-and-donkeys

VERSATILITY

https://www.youtube.com/watch?v=ww7wK2YSOHw&feature=youtu.be&fbclid=IwAR3XCGuZc6z9Hl-wQorj4_b_s6GSLxAysH6WcPqasTeo4p0x3KICAKDe4BSI
https://www.newsweek.com/fight-california-wildfires-mules-modern-technology-firefighters-1068010

TACK
https://americanmuleassociation.org/behaviortack-management
https://animals.mom.me/pack-mule-9165.html
https://www.muleranch.com/mule-saddle-everything-you-need-to-know/
http://www.the7msnranch.com/2011/05/mule-bars.html

MULE HISTORY
*https://www.mulemuseum.org/history-of-the-mule.html
http://imh.org/exhibits/online/breeds-of-the-world/africa/donkey/
http://imh.org/exhibits/online/breeds-of-the-world/europe/mule/
http://angelajanehoward.com/the-royal-jack-and-the-knight-of-malta/
*https://www.columbiadailyherald.com/article/20120328/LIFESTYLE/303289941
https://worldhistory.us/medieval-history/the-use-of-the-ass-mule-and-horse-in-medieval-travel.php
*http://mulography.co.uk/10-images-of-mules-in-history/
http://www.humanist.de/rome/rts/horse.html
https://abbeymedievalfestival.com/2012/06/the-medieval-horse/
http://animalhistorymuseum.org/exhibitsandevents/online-gallery/gallery-8-animals-and-empire/enter-gallery-8/i-imperial-species/mules/
http://animalhistorymuseum.org/cxhibitsandevents/online-gallery/gallery-8-animals-and-empire/enter-gallery-8/i-imperial-species/mules/
Pilgrimage to Rome in the Middle Ages: Continuity and Change by Debra Julie Birch
https://www.historyfiles.co.uk/KingListsMiddEast/CanaanOutremer.htm
https://www.medievalists.net/2019/07/warfare-during-crusades/
http://dariocaballeros.blogspot.com/2019/07/e-codices-illustrated-chronicle-by.html
https://www.soas.ac.uk/history/conferences/previous/donkey-conference---collected-papers-from-previous-conferences/file98154.pdf Donkeys and mules in the 'New World' John Barker
https://www.horsenation.com/2012/09/10/horses-in-history-george-washingtons-mule-fetish/
The Illustrated London News, August 20, 1864
The Moors in Spain by Stanley Lane-Poole, 1896
http://larryeifert.com/2017/09/14/mules-and-horses-santa-fe-trail-painting-for-the-national-trails-system/
https://www.parks.ca.gov/?page_id=25449
https://en.wikipedia.org/wiki/San_Antonio%E2%80%93San_Diego_Mail_Line
https://truewestmagazine.com/the-jackass-mail/
http://sweetheartsofthewest.blogspot.com/2015/09/war-hero-and-humanitarian-general.html
https://www.bishopvisitor.com/50th-anniversary-of-mule-days-in-bishop/ mule days

https://publishing.cdlib.org/ucpressebooks/view?docId=ft758007r3&chunk.id=d0e10744&toc.id=d0e10615&brand=ucpress
https://www.americancowboy.com/people/where-did-it-come-mules
https://truewestmagazine.com/the-history-of-mules/
https://www.historynet.com/6-million-mules.htm
http://clevelandcivilwarroundtable.com/articles/means/wagon_trains.htm
https://www.deseret.com/2009/7/13/20328732/salt-lake-streets-have-seen-many-changes-over-past-150-years
https://books.google.com/books?id=MaE5AQAAMAAJ&pg=PA865&lpg=PA865&dq=turning+a+6+horse+hitch+in+the+old+west&source=bl&ots=hb9JnTRkOA&sig=ACfU3U023V5YI9gD9ylMBDDz9u0qm75C-4A&hl=en&sa=X&ved=2ahUKEwi73630otHnAhVoFjQIHc0CDc4Q6AEwFHoECAsQAQ#v=onepage&q=addicted&f=false
https://www.tandfonline.com/doi/pdf/10.1080/10630730802097765
Joel A. Tarr & Clay Mcshane (2008) The Horse as an Urban Technology, Journal of Urban Technology, 15:1, 5-17, DOI: 10.1080/10630730802097765
https://www.worldwar1centennial.org/index.php/the-animals/3231-test-article-for-mules.html
https://www.worldwar1centennial.org/index.php/the-animals/3231-test-article-for-mules.html WWI
https://missouriorverthere.org/explore/articles/missouri-horses-and-mules/ WWI
https://nationalserviceanimalsmonument.org/mules/
https://www.worldwar1centennial.org/index.php/the-animals.html
https://warfarehistorynetwork.com/2016/01/29/army-mules-the-beast-of-burden-in-war/
https://www.mulemuseum.org/u-s-army-mules.html
https://www.csmonitor.com/USA/Military/2009/0504/p22s01-usmi.html
https://www.americanspecialops.com/photos/special-forces/special-forces-donkey.php

MULE STORIES
https://www.horsenation.com/2017/11/15/smokey-joe-the-clumsiest-surefooted-mule-in-the-world/
https://americanmuleassociation.org/storiesarticles
http://mulography.co.uk/four-mules-in-mythology/
https://www.wbur.org/onlyagame/2016/09/09/virl-pierce-norton-horse-mule-race
http://virlnorton.madmoosestudio.com/photos.php?album=2
http://www.aboutnorthgeorgia.com/ang/The_Lightning_Mule_Brigade
https://en.wikipedia.org/wiki/John_T._Wilder
https://civilwartalk.com/threads/lightning-mule-brigade.83821/
https://www.civilwarpoetry.org/union/battles/mules-exp.html

http://companyqdispatches.blogspot.com/2012/03/amusing-story-charge-of-mule-brigade.html
https://www.army.mil/article/16624/mule_bombs_at_valverde
https://www.desertusa.com/desert-people/paddy-graydon.html
http://exploringoffthebeatenpath.com/Battlefields/ForgottenFront/index.html
https://www.fold3.com/page/642791606-using-mules-in-burma/
https://www.ww2gp.org/3mulesInGlider.html
http://www.chindit.net/Mules.html
https://www.academia.edu/6616433/Burmas_Longeared_Paratroops
https://www.historylink.org/File/8651
https://www.tate.org.uk/art/artworks/bauchant-the-funeral-procession-of-alexander-the-great-t00466
https://www.theatlantic.com/technology/archive/2013/09/there-is-a-man-wandering-around-california-with-3-mules/279495/
http://horsefame.tripod.com/francis.html
https://www.findagrave.com/memorial/95415289/the_talking-mule-francis
http://www.randyspecktacular.com/2011/06/ode-to-mule.html
https://muledays.org/
https://www.horsenation.com/2019/02/20/5-truths-about-riding-mules/
https://www.dropbox.com/sh/yk30dy5dsyjlmx7/AAAzt6dNN8NolBauUH4SmNk3a?dl=0

www.ingramcontent.com/pod-product-compliance
Ingram Content Group UK Ltd.
Pitfield, Milton Keynes, MK11 3LW, UK
UKHW061139180426
11947UKWH00002B/5